Foster
and
Adoptive
Parenting

Authentic Stories
that Will Inspire and Encourage Parenting
with Connection

Kenneth A Camp

FREE RESOURCES!

Are you considering Foster Care or Adoption? Read this FREE ebook first! *Count the Cost*. Download it at www.kennethacamp.com/CounttheCost

You can also take a Free course based on this book. Sign up for the course at www.kennethacamp.com/CounttheCostCourse

Do you want to discover your mission in life? Download this FREE ebook—*21 Ways to Discover Your Mission*—www.kennethacamp.com/21Ways

In memory of Dr. Karyn Purvis

whose legacy continues to impact thousands of

children who "come from a hard place."

TABLE OF CONTENTS

CHAPTER ONE

Inspiration and Encouragement to Keep on Parenting with Connection

It's not uncommon for a parent who at one time was fully committed to fostering or adoption to feel so overwhelmed, alone, and discouraged that they begin thinking the unthinkable.

"Maybe I made a mistake." "Is this not the right child for our family?" "I don't think I can survive another day like this one!"

Even though many foster and adoptive parents have read the books on Parenting with Connection, attended seminars, sat in on classes, and even been in support groups, they feel themselves slipping into survival mode. What they hoped would bring joy and fulfillment feels as if it will destroy them.

They default to a parenting style that probably worked with them when they were a child or with their biological children but which they know probably won't work with kids from a hard place. The last thing they need is to parent in a way that only makes the situation worse.

I know these emotions are real. How do I know? I have felt them. My wife has felt them too. My friends who foster and adopt children also express these emotions.

The challenge is remembering the principles of Parenting with Connection when you are in the **middle** of the chaos—that's if you have learned them in the first place. When you learn these techniques in a book or a class, they don't always come to mind when you are in the thick of the mess.

Or maybe you do remember and apply them the best you can but you see little or no change. You might even feel that things get worse. You begin feeling less connected to your child, and you worry that things will never improve.

Foster and Adoptive Parenting will give you hope by not only teaching Parenting with Connection principles but mainly by giving you real-life examples of how to apply them. You will get encouragement that you are not alone in your struggle. You will get inspiration to keep on Parenting with Connection, because you will read and hear about other foster and adoptive parents who succeed and fail at times at Parenting with Connection.

Danielle and I never had our own children. Then, after 20-plus years of marriage, we decided to get foster care certified with the objective of adopting. We got our one and only foster placement (so far) of an eight-month-old boy in the summer of 2011. He was a foster-only placement, which means his biological family was working toward reunification. That never happened, and 15 months later we adopted our son.

So we can share stories from when our son was young and a foster child. And we can share some more from after we adopted him until his current age of about six.

We have read books, watched videos, and taken classes. In fact, we are certified trainers for Empowered to Connect, an intensive course that teaches foster and adoptive parents how to apply Parenting with Connection principles. Our soft cover copy of *The Connected Child* by Purvis and Cross is tattered and just about every sentence is underlined.

To give you the opportunity to hear from some other families, I have reached out to a few who vulnerably share some of their stories. These families also apply Parenting with Connection principles.

Each chapter takes Parenting with Connection tools taught by the experts and wraps them with real-life stories of struggle, failure, or success.

In this book you will find not only real-life application of parenting techniques and principles that you probably have already learned but you will also get the following:

- Links to audio podcast episodes where Danielle and I discuss in more detail some of the successes and failures our family has had when applying Parenting with Connection. Topics include how we handle transitions, the struggle our son had in attaching to us, and and how we handle Time In rather than Time Out.

- Links to audio podcast episodes of interviews with experts in this field on the topics of The Circle of Security parenting model, Sensory Processing, Attachment Style of the Parent, and The Importance of Taking Care of Yourself.

- References and links to helpful resources, such as, websites, articles, books, and videos.

I promise that if you engage with this book, not just read but engage, you will find the help, encouragement, and support that you are looking for.

Through the real-life examples and the audio interviews, I hope the Parenting with Connection principles will come alive for you.

Don't be that parent that isolates and burns out to the point that you consider throwing in the towel. We know these kids need us. We know they are worth the struggle. And we *all* know that it really *is* a struggle—a messy one.

What you are about to read and listen to will help you not only know how to apply Parenting with Connection strategies that will help your child from a hard place heal but also help you feel encouraged and supported.

You made the decision to foster or adopt a child. Make the decision to do your very best to help them heal and mature. Join others who are in the trenches with you.

The most important thing to do is to reach out and get support. I know that can be hard, but please know that you aren't alone—or you don't have to be. So promise me that if you don't read this book or use it as a tool to help you, you will use this encouragement to connect with other parents who understand your challenges.

CHAPTER TWO

It's Real Now

We all put on our Sunday best. We wanted to look good for the special day even though our not-quite-two-year-old, about-to-be-forever son didn't understand what the occasion was about. He was just excited to see the judge.

In his mind, the judge was going to be the judge from *Thomas the Train*, and that sounded delightful.

Family and friends met us in the huge, intimidating hallway of the county courthouse. Many didn't realize that all around us was sorrow and pain as people waited for their own court case. Many in the hallway and in the courtroom attended that day for reasons much less joyful than ours.

We came to celebrate.

The day at the courthouse reminded me of a wedding ceremony. We stood in front of the judge as our lawyer led us through a series of vows. Our family and friends stood with us as witnesses to this momentous day.

Then it was done. He was a part of our family forever.

Now it was party time. First we had a small after-the-court-hearing gathering at our home that was topped off with a gigantic cookie cake. Then a few days later, we had a huge party at a local park with food, cake, and presents. Our son still didn't know exactly the purpose of all the celebrating, but that park is still one of his favorites.

To top it off, we had one more party in the Houston area for family and friends. So more food, more cake, and, yes, more presents.

Then after we loaded up the presents, cleaned up the cake, and everyone went home, the parties were over. Even though it had been 15 months since Child Protective Services had placed our son in our home as a foster child, it hit me.

He was mine. Forever. **It was real now.**

We got an introduction to Dr. Karyn Purvis, and Parenting with Connection, months before we ever had a child in our home. We had just decided to get certified as foster parents, and a friend recommended that we attend a conference that was in town. The speaker? Dr. Karyn Purvis.

We had no idea at the time how unique an opportunity this was for us. I didn't even know who Dr. Karyn Purvis was. But there we were in a room with about 200 people for an entire day listening to her teach about a way of parenting—Parenting with Connection.

Dr. Purvis shared about how a child from a "hard place" needed to heal from the trauma experienced in their life. Yes they needed correction too, but until these children learned how to trust and how to overcome fear, any attempt to correct probably would fail.

We bought her book, *The Connected Child*, and began reading it. But it was only a theory for me until we had a child in our home, which didn't happen for over a year after that conference.

By that time, I had forgotten much of what I had heard at that conference and what I had read in the book, but we soon picked the book up off the bookshelf and read it through with a new set of eyes.

If we are not on the same page about Parenting with Connection, this book might frustrate you more than help. So let's take a moment and find out if we are talking the same language. Let's take a look in this next chapter to see what Parenting with Connection is exactly.

CHAPTER THREE

What Is Parenting with Connection?

"You know, what you really need to do with your kid is this" "When you were that age, this is how I handled your misbehavior"

We have all heard comments like these. When it comes to parenting, we get advice just about anywhere and from anyone—parents, grandparents, friends (even if they don't have kids!), experts, teachers, books, seminars, videos, and even Pinterest.

We try one approach hoping it will make our kids do the right thing. When it doesn't, we keep looking, and the odds are, we will find someone suggesting the exact opposite approach, and because we want our children to behave, we give that one a try too.

So how is Parenting with Connection not just another approach?

It *won't* be any different if you are looking for a quick fix like immediate behavior modification. Parenting with Connection isn't just a set of skills. *Any* parenting style or approach without connection is lacking.

Understanding four basic styles of parenting will help further define Parenting with Connection.

1. Authoritative—This seeks a balance between the child's need for independence and the parents need for obedience. These parents are very nurturing and very structured.

2. Permissive—This style is much more nurturing than structured. Often this style causes confusion for the child since expectations are lacking.

3. Authoritarian—This is characterized by high structure and low nurture by parents.

4. Uninvolved—An uninvolved parent provides barely any structure and doesn't nurture hardly at all. This borders on neglect.

Parenting with Connection takes an Authoritative approach. You are the boss. You have the power. You choose to share your power with your child. The key is finding a healthy balance between structure and nurture.

Discipleship

Parenting with Connection is like discipleship. If you aren't familiar with that word, it comes from the same root word as discipline—disciple. You disciple your child, meaning that you train your child to follow you with his whole being and heart.

Discipling your child involves a long-term approach instead of immediate behavior modification. You place value on your child's voice, needs, wants, etc., and you pay attention to your whole child, not just their behavior.

Connect, Empower, Correct

Parenting with Connection teaches you to Connect and Empower your child before you Correct them. Many parenting models focus on behavior modification which switches the order. Instead of Connect, Empower, and then Correct, you Correct, Empower, *then* maybe Connect. Or Correct, Correct, and Correct some more.

However the Parenting with Connection model puts an emphasis on *Connection*. Before you say that sounds more like Permissive parenting, remember that Parenting with Connection is high nurture and high structure.

Here is an example to help wrap your brain around the idea of high nurture and high structure:

My son and I like to explore around the five acres we live on. He collects sticks, finds treasure, and pretends we are fighting off any bad guys we encounter. I let him take the lead as I follow him all over. We dig around a hole to see if an animal lives in it (Yikes!) Then we take off across a field before the bad guys spot us. Up into the tree house we climb while using the sticks we collected earlier as weapons.

We connect through play like this. I enter his world and give him a voice.

But when he throws rocks my direction, I playfully tell him that rocks are not for throwing at people. If he stops, we continue the exploration and play.

I tell him that I will hold the sticks while he climbs into the tree house to which he responds with a little defiance, "I can climb up with the sticks!"

I respond with, "Are you telling me or asking me?" to which he replies, "Can I carry the sticks up the ladder, Daddy?"

"No son, it's not safe, but I will hand them to you as soon as you get up the ladder."

In this scene, my son feels nurtured as I enter his world, share my power with him, and give him a voice. At the same time, I provide high structure in that I don't allow him to do things that are not safe or disrespectful.

The objective of Parenting with Connection is building trust and attachment with your child. Regardless of what age a child is when they become a part of your family, they need to build trust and attachment with you.

Often this will mean parenting and loving on them as you would an infant or toddler. All children need the nurturing we naturally give a small child, such as rocking them, stroking their head, and so on.

To read an excellent article on the Focus on the Family website that goes into more depth on this topic, go to www.kennethacamp.com/Attachment.

If you give birth to your child, then you, especially moms, already have a unique connection. We strengthen that connection as we hold our babies and meet their every need. We don't scold them for crying, fussing, or making messes—unless we have some serious issues ourselves.

However, when they reach about eighteen months old, we begin modifying their behavior. They now can crawl, pull up on objects, and even walk around to explore their worlds. They are learning how to communicate with words like "No!" or "Mine!"

Before we know it, if we aren't careful, we are correcting more and more and connecting less and less.

If your child comes to you through foster care or adoption, they *need* for you to focus on connecting with them above anything else. You know that you will meet their basic needs like food, a place to sleep, and safety, but at first they don't know this. Even after they can intellectually see that this is true, it will take some time for them to *feel* this to be true.

During this period of time, which is different for each child, it is vital that we parent with equal parts of high nurture along with firm, consistent, yet gentle structure.

The goal for Parenting with Connection is to bond with your child. Again not just when they are a baby but all through their growing up years. When trust is built between you and your child, they develop a secure attachment so that when they begin to venture out into the world, they are not swayed by what the world is trying to teach them is right and wrong. They trust that what you have taught them is right and wrong. They are able to relate to others well and make healthy decisions on their own.

You have discipled them.

Trauma Informed Care

Any child that comes to us through foster care or adoption comes from a background of trauma, even if they are handed to us minutes after birth. For these kids, Parenting with Connection is even more important. You have been given not only the responsibility to raise this child well but also to help them heal. Correcting them without connecting will never help them heal. In fact, it can do even more harm.

What are developmental risk factors for a child, and why do these have an impact on the way you parent?

The TCU Institute for Child Development in their research on Trust Based Relational Intervention (TBRI) have identified six developmental risk factors:

1. **Prenatal stress or harm**—stress (even minimal amounts negatively affect the baby's

neurochemistry), substance use during pregnancy, domestic violence, homelessness, lack of prenatal care, lack of optimal nutrients, etc.

2. **Difficult labor or birth**—birth complications, emergency C-section, premature birth, or a lack of oxygen for any length of time

3. **Early medical trauma**—spending time in NICU

4. **Neglect**—failure to meet the child's emotional and physical needs, which communicates, "You don't exist"

5. **Abuse**—includes emotional, physical, and sexual abuse and communicates, "I don't like you"

6. **Traumatic event**—when a child experiences or witnesses something that causes a risk, or a perceived risk, of injury to themselves or others which causes extreme fear and helplessness

As you can see, any child, even one you gave birth to, can experience one or more developmental risk factors. Definitely every child that is placed in foster care or is adopted experiences one or more. Yes, even if the child you adopted was placed in your arms moments after being born, they, at the very least, experience loss.

Over the past 10–15 years, research has taught us a lot about what happens to a child's brain chemistry when they experience trauma (all the risk factors involve trauma).

Briefly, when a child experiences trauma, especially before age two, the amygdala overdevelops. This small part of the brain at the base of the skull is where our basic instincts reside. This part of the brain is fully developed by the time a child is born. Events that might seem normal to most easily cause a fear response from a child who is always in fight, flight, or freeze mode.

This child can "know" they are safe, or have enough to eat, or that you will never leave them, but they don't "feel" that way because of the altered chemistry in their brain.

The good news is that their brains can heal or "rewire". And you as their parent or caretaker can and are a huge part of that healing process—if you know what you are doing and do it well.

So again, the reason for this book is to not just teach these principles, because you can go to the experts for more in-depth teaching. My objective in this book is to encourage you to keep at it even when you feel like a failure or have no idea what to do.

Ready to dive in and look at some Connecting principles? One of the most important things to remember is that your child responds to his or her environment with fear. The question is how will we as parents respond to our children's fear-based behavior? In the next chapter, find out how I succeed and fail at this.

CONNECTION

"A child whose behavior pushes you away is a child who needs connection before anything else."
—*Kelly Bartlett, Encouraging Words for Kids*

CHAPTER FOUR

Responding to
Your Child's Fear

After 20-plus years of marriage without kids, I got used to uninterrupted conversation around the dinner table. Then enter a third party, a little person who feels left out when we don't include him.

I work on having age-appropriate conversation, but many times I notice that he is not really listening. Then, sure enough, he will ask, "What did you say?"

Other times he is playing with toys across the room while Danielle and I talk. He will chime in somewhere in the conversation revealing that he not only hears us but is listening to everything we say.

Another thing that I find interesting is that our son notices everything. He notices small details, who is in a room, what people wear, and what is missing. He has been doing this since he could talk.

A common daily question my son asks us is "What are we doing tomorrow?"

My son is typically in constant motion—jumping, running, and bouncing. He invades others' personal space and ramps up easily when excited. Is there a common underlying cause for these behaviors?

Often we misinterpret our child's behavior as rebellion or defiance. Instead, our child is reacting out of fear. Many times what gets labeled as hyperactivity is really hyper vigilance.

Here is a story from an adoption blogger friend, Sandra, about how her son's psychiatrist wanted to treat what he diagnosed as hyperactivity:

"When we entered someone's home, our four-year-old son's eyes darted around the room, taking in everything. He evaluated his surroundings in a matter of seconds: How many people were in the room? Did they look safe? How would he protect himself? No one left or even changed locations without him noticing".

"His psychiatrist wanted to put our son on ADHD medication as he said, 'Look at him. He is looking at everything in my office, and he is sitting on the edge of his seat ready to run.' Our son wasn't hyperactive. He was afraid."

How we respond can either help our child feel safe or make the situation worse.

Have you ever been afraid? Of course you have! What do you do when you are afraid? Have you ever run in circles and then done something really spastic? Do you obsessively scan your surroundings for any sign of danger?

What if you experienced chronic fear that put you in a constant state of alert? Would you be able to handle even the most basic tasks of life? How well would you relate to others? Could you listen to someone talking to you when your brain is in major alert mode? Could you even contemplate making plans for the future besides plans for survival?

Many of our children come to us in a constant state of alert. If you have a child that spent years in foster care or in an orphanage, they have merely learned how to survive.

A hyper-vigilant child constantly scans their environment for anything that looks or feels like a threat. Simple tasks such as listening, focusing, and being still take a back seat to the child being on high alert. This creates challenging behavior patterns.

If a child has continually lived in a state of chronic fear, maybe for years, the result is Post Traumatic Stress Disorder (PTSD).

A study (www.kennethacamp.com/PTSD) published in 2005 found that foster children are almost twice as likely to suffer from PTSD as U.S. war veterans are.

How Do We Respond to Hyper-Vigilance?

Dr. Jon Burgeron of Hope for Orphans says it like this: "The primary goal is not right behavior. It is relationship." He adds, "You have to do the right thing for a long time in order for a child from a hard place to feel safe."

That's the key with hyper-vigilant behavior. Your child might *know* they are safe. They might know they have all the food they will ever need. Intellectually they might reason that you won't abandon them, because you tell them these facts. But until they *feel* safe, *feel* like they have enough food, and *feel* that they won't be abandoned, they will remain on high alert, and their behavior will reflect this.

The sad thing is I know this about our son, and yet I still sometimes react in ways that only cause more fear.

For example, one evening as we went through our nighttime routine, my son pushed several of my buttons with his defiant, sassy attitude until I finally had had enough. I gave him two swift pops on his bottom and told him to "Straighten up!"

He darted away from me with fear-stricken eyes. With any move I made toward him, even as I tried to talk to him with a pleasant demeanor and a calm voice, he ran from me.

He didn't feel safe. He felt afraid. Admitting this to you makes my heart hurt.

Then here is what happened another evening (I see a pattern here—evening time when we are all tired):

Our son got very angry with Danielle. He got so mad that he didn't want anything to do with me either. He yelled at me that he didn't love me and didn't want me to touch him. Then he began to hit me and threatened to throw things at me. I calmly helped him regulate and talked about what was bothering him, and we made a transition to the bathtub to get ready for bed. After a few minutes of him in the bathtub, he called out for me.

I went to see what he needed. My son sat relaxing in the tub obviously deep in thought. He said, "Dad, I have been thinking."

"Okay," I replied.

He went on, "You know how you tell me that if I am always battling other people, I miss out on fun five-year-old stuff?"

"Yeah."

"And if I keep battling other people, I will miss out on six-year-old fun stuff too?"

"Yeah," I answered as I took a seat on the toilet after realizing that this was not going to be a short conversation.

He continued, "Well, I have decided to stop battling people so that I won't miss out on the fun stuff." I tried to keep a straight face as I told him that I thought that was a great idea!

I thought to myself, *I think he finally is beginning to feel safe enough that he doesn't feel like he has to fight the "bad guys" all the time. He can relax and enjoy being a normal five-year-old boy.*

Dr. Karyn Purvis talks in a video, The Impact of Fear (www.kennethacamp.com/ImpactofFear), about the importance of understanding how deep the fear level is for children from a hard place.

Takeaways from Dr. Purvis

- **Understand the toll of fear** on your child.

- **Learn to recognize fear** in your child. As Dr. Purvis points out in the video, does your child clench his fists, and are his eyes dilated or his breathing shallow? These are some tangible signs that your child is reacting to his environment from a place of fear.

- **Regulate stressors.** Stress elevates cortisol in our bodies, and this leads to hyperactivity. As a caregiver, remember this and preempt stressors when possible. They are never too young to teach deep breathing skills, pressure points, etc.

> *"By helping your child feel safe, making his or her world more predictable, and teaching better coping skills, you can actually optimize cortisol levels and allow your child's brain to work better."*
> —Dr. Karyn Purvis, The Connected Child

- **Help with transitions.** Transitions contribute to stress. Transitions from one activity to another, from one location to another, and from one phase of life to another are all examples of transitions. I talk more about this in a later chapter.

- **Teach your child how to trust** rather than to fear. The longer a child lives in fear the more it becomes their natural response to life. Earn a child's trust in the following ways:

  - Showing consistent emotional warmth and affection

  - Offering positive praise often

  - Responding attentively and kindly to your child's words

  - Interacting playfully

  - Being sensitive to your child's tolerance to sounds

- Respecting your child's need for personal space

- Using simple words they understand

- **Allow your child to talk about his fears.** I know this seems counterintuitive, but the more they talk about their fears, concerns, and even trauma, the better their brain integrates. As their brain integrates, they develop the ability to respond to their environment in a more rational manner rather than always in a fight, flight, or freeze mode.

> *"Children whose parents talk with them about their experiences tend to have better access to the memories of those experiences. Parents who speak with their children about their feelings have children who develop emotional intelligence and can understand their own and other people's feelings more fully."*
> *—Daniel J. Siegel, The Whole-Brain Child*

Are you thinking about how you respond to your child's fear-based behavior? As parents we need to do some detective work sometimes before we react to our child's behavior. If we notice signs of fear, we need to respond in a way that helps them feel safe. Otherwise, any attempt to correct is a waste of time.

In the next chapter I share a story of my son's expressionless response as he watched his biological parents walk away. That memory still haunts me to this day. Do you know what that meant? It reflected a disorganized attachment to his biological parents. The question is how do we as foster or adoptive parents deal with a child with a disorganized or less than secure attachment style?

CHAPTER FIVE

Securing Your Child's Attachment

I remember taking our son to his first parent visit at the Child Protective Services (CPS) office. He had only been with us a couple of days. His biological parents were both young and unmarried, and they didn't have a place of their own. They lived either with her parents or his. So in the short eight months of this child's life, he had moved around a lot.

When we walked through the double glass doors, we could see his parents standing waiting to hold their son. His young mother held out her arms with a huge smile on her face, and I carefully handed him over to her.

At the time I didn't notice his response—or lack of it. But when we left the parent visit an hour later, I couldn't help but notice it.

We were parked on opposite sides of the building. I had our son in my arms with his head looking over my shoulder, and I could see his face as he watched his biological parents walk the other way.

I would expect a child securely attached to his parents to cry and hold out his hands as he watched his parents walk away from him, especially when he hadn't seen them in a couple of days.

However, he just stared at them with a blank look on his face. I didn't fully understand at the time what happened there, but it broke my heart. I now understand that this little baby boy was not securely attached to them.

If you think that is a unique story, here is a story Sandra told about their foster son:

"Our son was placed with us when he was 17 months old. At the court hearing the day after his placement with us, my husband and I rode in the elevator with a man who introduced himself and had a brief conversation with us. We soon found out that this was our foster son's biological father. Our son didn't so much as acknowledge his biological father's presence. At the time I thought to myself, *Aw our foster son has already learned to love my husband. I was so naive.*"

Attachment Dance

I like to dance, and I am pretty good at it . . . for about three beats. Then I tense up. Just ask my wife, Danielle. Because when we are doing the two-step (we are from Texas!), and I get off beat, I squeeze her hand out of frustration. It's not exactly a way to nurture a good relationship.

Attachment is a lot like a dance. Some are good at it. Others not so much. Raising a son who comes from a hard place teaches me a lot about attachment—not only his but mine also.

So that we are talking the same language, let's take a moment to describe attachment styles.

Here are the four basic attachment styles briefly defined:

- **Secure**

Children who are securely attached generally become visibly upset when their caregivers leave and are happy when their parents return. When frightened, these children will seek comfort from the parent or caregiver.

While these children can be comforted to some extent by other people in the absence of a parent or caregiver, they clearly prefer parents to strangers.

- **Ambivalent**

Children who are ambivalently attached tend to be extremely suspicious of strangers. These children display considerable distress when separated from a parent or caregiver but do not seem reassured or comforted by the return of the parent. In some cases, the child might passively reject the parent by refusing comfort or may openly display direct aggression toward the parent.

- **Avoidant**

Children with avoidant attachment styles tend to avoid parents and caregivers. This avoidance often becomes especially pronounced after a period of absence. These children might not reject attention from a parent, but neither do they seek out comfort or contact. Children with an avoidant attachment show no preference between a parent and a complete stranger.

• **Disorganized**

Children with a disorganized-insecure attachment style show a lack of clear attachment behavior. Their actions and responses to caregivers are often a mix of behaviors, including ambivalent or avoidant. These children are described as displaying dazed behavior, sometimes seeming either confused or apprehensive in the presence of a caregiver.

In normal environments, 60% have secure attachments, 20% are ambivalent, and 20% are avoidant. Only 2% to 3% are disorganized. However, according to many studies, as much as 80% in the high-risk child population are disorganized.

Studies also show that a child establishes their primary attachment style by the time they are age five or six. The good news is that any child, or adult for that matter, can change their attachment style. This is called Earned Secure Attachment.

I learned that I had an avoidant attachment style, and, I hope, I now have an earned secure attachment style. I talk more about this in chapter 23, "Paying Attention to What You Bring."

The Struggle Our Son Had to Attach to Us

During the first two to three years that our son was in our family, he did a couple of things that reflected a disorganized attachment style.

One thing our son did I called the Trauma Dance. Whenever he got hurt, instead of running to Danielle or me, he ran around in circles as if he was looking for a safe place to receive comfort.

Once when I was out of town on a trip something happened to our son that upset him. He cried and yelled that he wanted his daddy even though Danielle stood right there trying to comfort him. Danielle gently explained that I wasn't there to comfort him but that she was there for him to which he loudly replied, "Any daddy will do!"

Another behavior that both amused and saddened us was how our son tried to go home with other families. This happened many times when he was around three years old. If we were at the park or a mall playground and he enjoyed playing with some other children, when they got ready to leave, he tried to join right in. I remember hearing him tell one family, "I want to go home with you guys." Danielle or I chased after him more than once telling him that we were his mommy and daddy and that he went home with *us*.

Building Trust with Our Kids

> "Children from hard places need to learn how to trust in order to heal. For this to happen, parents must move in closer even as their child pushes them away. They must resolve conflict and respond to misbehavior in ways that both correct and connect. This often requires parents to connect first, then correct—an approach that goes against the instincts of most parents, but actually can make their correction even more effective."
>
> —Michael Monroe, *When Your Child Pushes You Away*

We know firsthand how hard it is to move in closer when your child avoids you or pushes you away. We experienced all kinds of emotions every time our son did this. It is better now, but he still pushes us away. I remember nights when Danielle cried herself to sleep wondering if our son would ever attach to her like a son does with his mommy.

When a couple or single decides to foster or adopt, we can believe the myth that all the child needs is our love. When our child rejects that love, we can respond with anger, confusion, disillusionment, sadness, and so on.

Danielle and I had to intentionally put aside those emotions and embrace our son. Sometimes we did this well; other times not so well.

I talk more in the last section of the book about self-awareness. The more we are aware of our own stuff, the more this will help us respond patiently to our kids.

Here is an important thing to remember:

We all are created to connect. We all seek relationships where we feel safe being ourselves. As a parent I can learn to create as safe a place as possible for my child to attach to me. This includes my state of calmness, my tone of voice, and my nonverbal communication, like the look on my face, my posture, my movement, and so on.

If you want to listen in to Danielle and me talk more about our sons struggle to attach to us, and some successes that we are seeing now, listen to this podcast— **"The Struggle to Attach." (http://kennethacamp.com/Episode12)**

We as foster and adoptive parents need to figure out how to help our children trust so that they can securely attach in relationships. In the next chapter, I will help you not only understand what the Circle of Security is, I will provide you some insight on how to make it work. A valuable part of that insight comes from a podcast interview with Suzette Lamb. You don't want to miss that.

CHAPTER SIX

Establishing a Safe Haven for Your Child

Attachment is such an important thing between a parent and a foster or adopted child that I want to make sure you are familiar with the Circle of Security parenting model.

Normally a child ventures out from the safe haven and secure base a parent provides to explore their world and then returns to their parent. This begins as soon as a child is born with what they explore with their eyes. They look into the loving face of a parent or caretaker then quickly look around to see what's in the world around them. After a few seconds they look back into the parent's face.

In those few seconds, they completed a Circle of Security.

The circle goes like this:

As a parent or caretaker, we give our child a secure base for them to launch their exploration. Our child needs us to support their exploration by watching over them, delighting in them, helping them, and enjoying them. Especially when our child is young, they need to feel as if they are the center of our universe.

Then as our child returns to our safe haven, they need us to welcome them home by protecting them, comforting them, delighting in them, and helping them organize their feelings.

We always are bigger, stronger, wiser, and kind. Whenever possible we follow their needs. Whenever necessary we take charge.

A young child usually will go around this circle several times in an hour especially if in a new environment. A teenager goes around the same circle of security, but it just looks a little different. Instead of the exploration lasting just a few minutes, it will be hours, days, or maybe even months at a time. But they still need us as parents to watch over them, delight in them, and help them when they need help. Eventually they will return home for protection, comfort, and processing.

Here is a diagram of the Circle of Security.

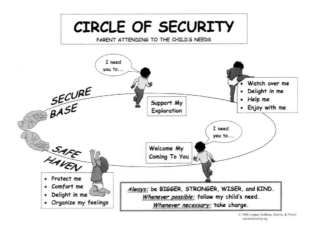

CIRCLE OF SECURITY

PARENT ATTENDING TO THE CHILD'S NEEDS

SECURE BASE

I need you to...

Support My Exploration

- Watch over me
- Delight in me
- Help me
- Enjoy with me

I need you to...

Welcome My Coming To You

SAFE HAVEN

- Protect me
- Comfort me
- Delight in me
- Organize my feelings

Always: be BIGGER, STRONGER, WISER, and KIND.
Whenever possible: follow my child's need.
Whenever necessary: take charge.

© 1998 Cooper, Hoffman, Marvin, & Powell
circleofsecurity.org

This short video (www.kennethacamp.com/COS) will give some more explanation about Circle of Security.

Not only did our son avoid coming to us when he hurt but often he took off running when in public places. For over a year any time we went to the mall or a park or a store, we had to talk through with him how we wanted him to stay with us. But on occasion I would find myself darting though the crowd trying not to lose sight of my slippery little three-year-old.

Sometimes it made me angry, especially when I had a sore ankle tendon that eventually tore. So you can imagine my emotional state when I finally caught up with him.

That might seem funny, but it's not normal for a child to run away from his parents without even looking back once.

As parents of adopted children or caretakers of foster children, our children very likely missed out on this Circle of Security. This is true whether they woke up as a baby in an orphanage with no one there to respond to their cries or if your child woke up each morning in an abusive or unpredictable home.

Sadly children from a hard place don't have the bigger, stronger, wiser, kind caretaker/parent in their life. For some, it might be for a few hours or days because of a neonatal medical cause. For others it is more chronic like abuse or neglect.

Did you know that when a parent knows or is decisive about what to do next with their child, the child gains confidence? It's called mirror neurons. A child will reflect or imitate our actions. If we are anxious and unsure, the child will be anxious and unsure. If we are calm and confident, then, well you get the idea.

Understanding the Circle of Security is so important that I asked my friend Suzette Lamb to expound on this some more for us. Suzette is a licensed professional counselor supervisor with clinical experience that includes group, individual, marital and family therapy. She has extensive training in attachment, adoption, and trauma. Before joining Central Texas Attachment and Trauma Center Suzette was the clinical director of a foster/adoptive agency for almost 20 years.

Suzette also has advanced training in the Circle of Security parenting model as a parent educator. Danielle and I had the privilege of attending a retreat where Suzette taught on this subject.

I share a few nuggets from the podcast interview here, but I recommend that you take the time to listen to the podcast episode by clicking on www.kennethacamp.com/session009.

Nuggets from Suzette Lamb Interview:

- This model applies to every parent/child relationship.

- Our goal as parents is to be a great launching pad and a warm safe place to return to.

- We want to raise children who have autonomy within relatedness and relatedness within their autonomy.

- As humans we are designed to be connected with other people. We need to know that others are concerned about us, interested in us, and available to us.

What I Have Learned About the Circle of Security

- I can tell at any moment where my son is on the circle—exploring his world, returning home, or in his safe haven. When I identify this, I can easily tell what he needs from me.

- My ability to provide a secure and safe haven for my son to return to will greatly determine how well he attaches to me.

- Secure parents can stand back and see what they are doing (and not doing) for their children.

- Secure parents can admit where they struggle and, for the sake of their children, work to find another way.

- I need to learn to be with my son just enough so that he feels like he is on his own.

I like that last one! I don't want my son to feel controlled, but I do want him to feel safe.

I know many parents struggle with parenting with connection because it seems too permissive and allows the child to dictate too much. These first three chapters in this section can feed that belief when we talk about understanding that our kids have fear-based responses, that they probably have an insecure or even disorganized attachment style, and they don't feel like they have a safe haven.

It's common for our compassion to kick in and respond to our children with a more permissive parenting style. But that is the last thing they need from us. What our kids need is a strong balance of lots of structure along with tons of nurture.

Let's dig into that a little more in the next chapter because if you are like me, you struggle with either one extreme or the other. But I know I can help you find the adequate balance.

CHAPTER SEVEN

Balancing Nurture and Structure for Your Child

I feel like a pendulum swing. You know the kind I am talking about—the one with six balls, each suspended by a string. When at rest they hang next to each other barely touching. Just hanging there. Balanced.

Then one ball from either end is pulled back. It bangs against the one next to it which bangs into the one next to it, and so on, until all six balls are swinging back and forth.

That's how I feel when I try to find the balance between nurture and structure. I keep striving for balance but end up banging into resistance. Then I just swing back and forth, back and forth.

I guess it's not bad that I try to find balance, but I sure wish it wasn't so hard sometimes.

Four Parenting Styles

Remember reading about the four parenting styles in Defining Parenting with Connection?

- Authoritative

- Permissive

- Authoritarian

- Uninvolved

To parent with connection, we need the balanced approach of Authoritative parenting. That is exactly the kind of parent described in the Circle of Security.

An authoritative parent is engaged, confident, strong, and kind.

High Nurture

I feel almost schizophrenic. One moment I am this calm, patient, nurturing dad. One picture that comes to mind is my son riding with me on the lawn tractor. He likes to steer it while I control the gas and brake. The only reason he doesn't tell me that he will do that too is because he can't reach it yet. When he can he will have earned a new chore.

But as we sit together on the tractor riding around the property, laughing and enjoying life, I feel the connection. I let him go wherever he wants to go within reason.

I love it when my son spontaneously calls out, "Daddy?" "Yes son?" "I love you." "I love you too buddy."

Those moments are worth me working to understand him, his past, and his fears. That connection is worth me focusing on connecting with him.

High Structure

I think I often misunderstand what high structure should look like. That's why I feel a little crazy sometimes. I can have a sweet moment like the one riding around on the lawn tractor; then, just a few moments later, my son will do something that sends me over the edge.

High structure isn't me doing anything that creates fear in my son. In my anger I can yell, threaten, pop him on the bottom, grab his arm—ugh. If we are honest as parents, we have all been there. Our buttons get pushed, and we don't respond like we want to.

Instead, high structure involves learning how to correct in ways that adequately match the misbehavior. (We will get into specific ways to provide high structure in later chapters.) I tend to overreact instead of respond.

A good question to ask is "Am I maintaining a connection, or restoring it quickly, when I correct my child?"

The challenge for me is my sense of justice and my need to correct misbehavior with rules, scolding, and punishments, like giving consequences. So I tend to parent from this side of the pendulum swing more often.

As a result, I then feel bad for how much I am correcting my son, and I will have a day where I am too permissive.

It's not just a balance of nurture and structure that our children from a hard place need. They need both *high* nurture and *high* structure.

I swing from one day being very nurturing to the next day being very structured. Some days its from hour to hour.

When done well, a balance of nurture and structure helps children in these ways:

- **It gives healthy boundaries.**

The children we parent need to know where the line is. When we consistently and compassionately show them where the line is, they will respond. It might take time for some, but it's important to remember that isn't because they want to rebel. They want to obey. Compassionately enforced healthy boundaries grow healthy relationships.

Everyone feels out of control and unsafe when we can't tell where our boundaries are. When a child responds to their environment out of fear, gently help them identify their boundaries to help them feel safe.

- **It builds trust.**

Because these children come from unpredictable environments, they don't know what to expect or whom to trust. That's why the temptation for some parents is to give high nurture with little structure. The parent thinks,

My kid has already suffered so much; they just need my loving.

That's true to some extent. But when we don't combine that high nurture with high structure, we fail to teach them what is expected of them. They fearfully react to a lack of structure. The firm, compassionate correction helps them know that they can rely on us to show them how to navigate and make sense of life. That builds trust.

- **It allows for age-appropriate behavior.**

I have heard foster kids described as street smart. It's a true description and can help them in life. But children need to know it's okay to enjoy life as a five-, 10-, or 15-year-old. When we as parents are the safe haven that they have lacked, and we appropriately demonstrate that we are bigger, stronger, wiser, and kinder than they are, they feel that they can let go and act their age.

If you can do this well—balancing high nurture with high structure—then the rest of the parenting with connection principles come easier. I know one thing: When I am always saying "No!" or even "No, NO, NOOOO!" I am not doing a very good job with this high nurture and high structure thing.

In this next chapter, we look at a couple of easy and fun ways to nurture your kid. You might be familiar with these principles, but how well are you doing with them?

I have a solution to help you say yes to your child in appropriate amounts. Ready to hear what it is? Our son loves it. I will also help you discover your play personality. Did you know that you have a play personality?

CHAPTER EIGHT

Why Can't We
Tell Our Kids Yes?

Our children respond to different ways of nurturing. As a parent, part of our detective work is knowing what fills our kid's emotional cup. These two tools, "Saying Yes" and "Taking Time to Play," work with any child and can help us fill their emotional cup. What is different for each child is the specific way we engage in saying yes or playing with them.

Saying Yes

I am really good at saying no. I can say it kindly, with force, in rapid succession, with anticipation of the question, and even without looking. In my mind, I always have a good reason for telling my son no. I don't want him to do that, eat those, or bother me at the moment.

I think I should invent an app like the ones that record every step you take so that you can see how many miles you incidentally walked in a day, except this app would record every time you say no to your child. On second thought, I don't think I want to know.

Why is it so hard for me to just say it? Just Say Yes.

I think I know why. I am afraid if I say yes too much it will ruin my son. Won't he grow up thinking that he can have anything he wants, do everything he wants, and never have to wait his turn?

When a Child Needs to Hear No

Of course, sometimes we need to tell our children no. This goes back to the appropriate balance of nurture and structure. It's our responsibility to keep our children safe, to make sure they get good nutrition, and to ensure that they learn to make good choices.

However, what I can learn to do better is how to say no in a way that still nurtures instead of in a way that squelches my son's spirit, comes across as a punishment, or even causes fear.

I can say no with playful interaction, with immediate praise for a good response, and with a kind voice and facial expression.

Once again, if my goal is behavior modification rather than connection along with a longterm result, then saying no with disregard to how often and how I say it will work fine.

Daddy or Mommy Yes Days

So what are these Daddy and Mommy Yes Days? This is another great idea we picked up from Dr. Purvis.

We decided to offset the number of times we say no to our son by having, on occasion, a day where we would say yes to any and every reasonable request our son made. These work well when it is a day when one of us is with him most of the day, and we don't have any set plans.

"Can I watch another TV show?" "Sure, just one more."

"Can we go to a park?" "You bet. We will go for a few minutes on our way to the store."

"Daddy, I want pizza for lunch." "Sounds good to me."

"Can you play this game with me?" "Can we read books?" "Can I have another treat?"

"Yes, yes, and yes."

After a Daddy Yes Day, I know why I sometimes say no more often than yes. It is easier, less time consuming, and not as exhausting.

It also takes more creativity on my part to think of ways to say yes, especially yes to things I am okay with approving. I will slow my response down a few seconds to ask myself, "Is there any reason I can't or don't want to say yes to this request?" If I can't think of a good reason, then it's "Yes."

As you can imagine, our son loves these days. From time to time he asks, "Can today be a Daddy Yes Day?" Now how can I say no to that cute face?

Two things happen when we have a Daddy Yes Day. First, I recognize how I often I say no just because. Second, my son and I connect more because I enter his world, I hear his requests, I give him a voice, and so on.

A connection tool that works well with Saying Yes is Taking Time to Play. Some parents are great at it. Others feel lost. The first step is to find out what your play personality is. Then it's all about taking the time to play.

Taking Time to Play

> *"Play can bring down the chemistry of fear and raise up the chemistry of healing in their brains."*
> —*Dr. Karyn Purvis*
>
>
> *"The opposite of play is not work. It is depression."*
> —*Dr. Stuart Brown*

I like to play. I like playing games, being silly, competing, pretending, and making jokes. What I didn't know is how hard playing can be sometimes.

I learned that there are many play personalities when I read Dr. Stuart Brown's book, *Play: How It Shapes the Brain, Opens the Imagination, and Invigorates the Soul,* which outlines eight play personalities. Which one(s) do you have?

- **The Joker**

The joker play personality represents the most obvious and often the most extreme style of playful parent. It is an inherently fun, silly, nonsensical style of play and can sometimes even be outrageous.

- **The Kinesthete**

The focus of this play personality is movement. This includes athletes and those who are most alive when they are on the move by walking, running, swimming, hiking, dancing, etc.

- **The Explorer**

Exploring is the preferred means of play for those with this play personality. Exploring can be physical (as in going to new places) or it can be intellectual (discovering new ideas or information), relational (meeting new people), or emotional (searching for a new response to music, art, or a story).

- **The Competitor**

This play personality enters the world of play through engaging in competitive games with the object of winning. This can be done in a small group setting (i.e., one-on-one with your child) or as part of a larger group (i.e., team sports/games).

- **The Director**

Planning, organizing, and orchestrating scenes and events are what marks this play personality. Homemade movies, amateur music recordings, planning a party, cooking a large meal for the holidays, and so much more are included in this style of play personality.

- **The Collector**

This play personality is all about assembling and/or maintaining a collection of interesting objects or experiences. Collecting can be done all alone or with others who have similar interests.

- **The Artist/Creator**

Making things is the focus and source of joy for this play personality. Think arts and crafts of virtually any kind as well as inventing, designing, decorating, and constructing. These creations can be functional, artistic, or simply playful.

- **The Storyteller**

This play personality focuses on imagination. It may be the predominant personality for those who love to read, write, draw cartoons, or watch movies. Those with this play personality are able to create an imaginative world that can permeate almost any activity or context.

Figuring Out What Works

I know that I have more than one play personality. The prominent ones are the Joker, the Kinesthete, and the Competitor. But I can't stop there for this to work. I need to learn what my son's play personality is too. I think it is the Joker, the Competitor and maybe the Director and the Explorer.

When my son initiates play with me it usually involves recreating a battle scene or building a magnificent castle. Even though those don't fall fully into my play personality, my son feels loved and nurtured when I engage him with play as he leads.

I hit a home run anytime I say yes to my son's request to play with him and especially when I let him lead. I find it is hit or miss if I initiate the play time. I guess that is because I often initiate play that fits my personality rather than his, and this puts me in control instead of him.

Then more often than I care to admit, I tell my son no to his requests to play. Sometimes my excuse is valid, such as I am working. But other times, I am "too tired" or "too busy." These are lost opportunities to connect with my son.

It reminds me of the song "Cat's in the Cradle" by Harry Chapin. One verse and the chorus go like this:

"My son turned ten just the other day. He said, "Thanks for the ball, Dad, come on let's play. Can you teach me to throw?" I said, "Not today I got a lot to do", He said, "That's okay" and he walked away but his smile never dimmed and said, "I'm gonna be like him, yeah, you know I'm gonna be like him."

And the cat's in the cradle and the silver spoon. Little boy blue and the man on the moon. When you comin' home, Dad?. I don't know when, but we'll get together then. You know we'll have a good time then.

The song goes on as the roles reverse with the dad asking the son to spend time with him but the son doesn't have time for his dad.

It's up to me to make sure our song turns out differently. Saying Yes and Taking Time to Play are work. I have to intentionally do these things, or the days turn into weeks, months, and eventually years.

I hope this chapter inspires you to go spend time with your children.

Well these last few chapters focused on ways to connect with your child. I find connecting with my son enjoyable when I learn ways to do it. But sharing my power with my son, especially when he is only five, is a different story.

If you have the same struggle, I am confident that in the next few chapters I can help you work out ways that you are comfortable with so that you can share power or empower your child. Don't worry. You are still the boss.

EMPOWERMENT

"When the children are young, then we as parents hold the power. And we can share it in appropriate amounts with our children. As our children get older, they have a significant amount of power. If I want my child to be competent with power at the age of 16, I have to teach them how to handle power at the age of four."[i]
—*Dr. Karyn Purvis*

CHAPTER NINE

Handling Transitions and Getting Your Child Moving

Transitions are a part of everyone's lives, and they usually cause all kinds of unregulated responses. Anxiety. Depression. Excitement. Even anger.

For kids who react to their environment out of fear, the uncertainty that transitions bring easily causes a big emotional response.

How Do We Handle Transitions?

When our son completed his second year of preschool, some past coping behaviors resurfaced—chewing on his shirt, separation anxiety, etc. We thought that he was past this behavior, and Danielle and I struggled to find the cause. Then on the next to last day of pre-school, he asked Danielle, "What if my teacher next year doesn't love me?"

We then understood that this was most likely the cause of his behavior. I knew most kids ramp up at the end of the school year and wonder what the next year will bring, but this took me a little by surprise.

Honestly, I was frustrated by his regressed behavior, especially his separation anxiety. I had to breathe deeply when he clung to my leg instead of going into his classroom. My lack of understanding caused my frustration, even though I shouldn't always need to understand. I know sometimes I never will understand. But it sure helps when I do.

His question revealed his heart to me, and reminded me that he needs my patience and gentleness. Knowing what is causing his anxiety helps me to at least try to discuss it and help ease it. He and I can talk about it, process it, and deal with it in a constructive way rather than him suffering and coping on his own.

Danielle and I know now how much chronic trauma affects the wiring of the brain resulting in chronic fear. Any child will struggle with transitions; however, if they feel safe and feel that their environment is predictable, then that child probably will handle transitions better. Understand that this won't eliminate your child's fear or challenging behavior, but it will help.

There are three main types of transitions:

1. ***Daily transitions***—Moving from one activity to another throughout the day is a challenge for a child who is fear-driven or in survival mode. A daily question, sometimes many times a day, which our son asks is, "What are we doing tomorrow?" If I don't plan well for these transitions—provide adequate warning, build in

extra time, and stay patient—I create a stressful environment for my son, which makes it more difficult for him to self-regulate.

2. *Major life transitions*—As I am writing this chapter, my son is about to begin kindergarten. It's a new school. None of his current friends will attend this school. New teachers. New routine. Talk about a major transition! His behavior the last few weeks reflect this too. The last thing I need to do is berate his behavior and tell him to not worry about it. Instead taking time to process the transition by letting him tell his story, drawing a picture that tells the story, etc. will help his brain reorganize around this bit of information and make sense of the transition.

3. *Developmental transitions*—We all have to learn how to navigate developmental transitions. In my 50s, my brain is reorganizing around the fact that my body doesn't recover as quickly as it did when I was in my 30s. For a young child these transitions come more often as they age. Our son is no longer an infant or a preschooler but is now quickly becoming a young child. Children need predictability and some level of control. Children, especially from a trauma background, benefit from family or daily rituals, such as getting up at the same time, eating meals around the same time, and having a similar nighttime process.

We can predict some transitions. Others catch us off guard. Either one can cause our kids to regress in behavior and struggle with regulation. Children aren't always able to know what to expect, but we as parents can prepare for transitions of all kinds. The better we think ahead, the better we can help our kids. Even if we are caught off guard, we can respond rather than react.

Danielle and I share more about our experiences with helping our son handle daily and major life transitions in this podcast episode. Either click or copy and paste this link to listen in on our conversation—**Helping Our Son Handle Transitions (www.kennethacamp.com/Episode6).**

Incorporating Movement into Times of Transition

If your child is struggling with transitions, whether they are daily, major life, or developmental, applying appropriate types of movement can empower them to successfully handle the transition.

As we looked to help our son navigate his major transition into kindergarten, I met with the school principal, the school counselor, and the kindergarten teacher at the beginning of the summer. It was music to my ears as they talked about the Trauma Informed Care training that many had taken. They understood how movement can help any child but especially kids that deal with trauma, fear, and sensory processing challenges.

They have things at the school like exercise balls to sit on, squeeze toys to fiddle with, and so on. If a child struggles with focusing, they will send him, along with an adult buddy, "on an errand" or to do a few laps and then bring the child back to class.

This type of movement will help our son make not only the transition to a new school but also through small transitions throughout the day.

I have a phlegmatic personality. If you're not familiar with that personality style, a card that Danielle got me once describes it well: "Why stand if you can lean. Why lean if you can sit. Why sit if you can lay down."

But that doesn't help my complex brain much. I need to get up and move. Not only does it help when I go for a walk when I work from home but it also helps me to go to the gym or play sports regularly.

As adults, we learn that it helps to get up and move around. It's almost second nature for me. When I have sat still for over an hour working on a project, I can feel the need to get up and move. When I worked in an office building, I regularly went up and down the stairs. Now that I often work from home, I will take a walk outside around my property. I didn't understand the physiology of the benefit until recently, but I experientially knew that it helped my cognitive abilities. Even though it seems counter-intuitive, getting our kids moving will also help them to think with the complex part of their brain rather than the fear-response part.

> *"Research shows that when we change*
> *our physical state—through movement*
> *or relaxation—we can change our emotional state."*
> *—Dan Siegel, The Whole Brain Child*

We do this pretty well around our house. When our son is unregulated, it's common for me to say to him, "Run and touch that tree, and come back" or "Jump 20 times on your mini-trampoline." He even has begun to do this on his own. The other day I looked out on our back porch that is the width of our house to see him running laps. He seems to know that it helps him calm down. I love it.

What Dan Siegel's quote from *The Whole Brain Child* revealed to me is that it isn't always just a physical activity that is necessary. It can be as simple as moving from one position to another.

I have seen this work with our son by having him move from one room to another even if it's to go play with Legos or read a book; neither involves a lot of movement, but the moving to another room and activity helps him to refocus and use the complex part of his brain.

On the other hand, some things, like wrestling, don't calm him down one bit. Sure we connect because he loves it, but he tends to get ramped up to the point that I have to move us to another activity so he can calm back down.

In the next chapter I touch on some ways we can empower our kids that often is overlooked. These simply are making sure that our children get enough sleep, water, and proper nutrition. I share some stories from our family and another that I am sure will give you some insight and solutions.

CHAPTER TEN

Sleeping, Drinking Water, and Eating

Sometimes we overlook some of the easiest ways to empower our kids, for example, our physiological state impacts how well our brains work. When we have a deficit of sleep, food, or water, we all, adults and children, struggle mentally.

Our children's poor or confusing behavior might simply be a result of a lack of sleep, food, or water. If we try to correct the behavior without meeting these basic needs first, we are wasting our time. When we continue to ignore their basic needs and focus on correcting their behavior instead, this tells them that they can't express their need for basic things, and it will eventually cause shame.

To help illustrate, I will share a couple of stories here. One story is from a family who fostered and eventually adopted two little girls who exhibited strange behavior because of fear (which we talked about in chapter 4) and lack of sleep and good nutrition.

The other story is one that I am sure many of you have experienced with your own child in a similar situation.

The question is, did you recognize the cause of your child's behavior?

Why Your Child Doesn't Sleep

Doctors in general recommend that children up to five years old get, on average, 10 hours of sleep each day. For a kid up to the age of 13, it's recommended they still get at least nine hours of sleep.

One of the most common challenges that a parent or caretaker of a foster or adopted child is presented with is sleep.

Do you ever wonder why our kids struggle with sleep? Read a part of Kirby and Carie's story of the first few nights after they began to foster two sisters.

Carie got a call in the middle of the afternoon while grocery shopping. The director of her child placing agency had a question for her. All Carie heard her tell her was that they had two little sisters, ages two and three, who had been waiting in their office since 11 that morning. They needed a place to stay the night.

When Kirby and Carie went to meet the girls, what they saw broke their hearts: two little girls who were obviously malnourished, especially the three-year-old.

Kirby and Carie agreed to foster the girls and took them home. The first couple of nights presented a challenge, though, when the oldest girl didn't want to go to bed.

"She still didn't speak, and her eyes darted around the room. She chewed everything. She even chewed the entire bottom rail of her bed. It looked like a beaver had gone to town on the railing, but there were no wood chips. Had she swallowed them? Did they just disappear? We told her if she chewed the railing again, we would have to take it off. The next night instead of chewing the railing, she chewed her fingertips until they bled."

What a heartbreaking story. This story clearly explains why our kids struggle with sleep. It is what we talked about in chapter 4. They are too afraid to sleep.

How did Carie and Kirby help their foster daughter? Even though she was three years old, they began from the beginning. They bonded with her as if she was their newborn.

Here is how Carie explains it:

"I bought her a pacifier and a bottle. I just knew in my gut that she needed some re-training and bonding. People ask, 'Why the paci and bottle? She's not a baby. Why would you go backwards?' Here's why. Children revert back to the age of trauma. She was acting like a baby, so I pulled out my old baby wrap and started wrapping her to me. I would wear her at least 30 minutes a day and usually two to three times a day. At night, my husband did the same thing. He thought I had lost my mind at first but when I explained what I thought was happening and what she needed, he agreed to try anything. Every time we put this sweet girl in our baby wrap she tried to tuck her knees up to her chest, and sometimes she even put her hands down my shirt, just like a baby would do. She would babble like a baby and would chew like crazy on her paci."

Carie and Kirby understood that they needed to help their foster daughter feel safe. And when she felt safe, she slept.

Your Kid Might Just Need to Eat or Drink Some Water

Recently my son and I spent the day together, just the two of us. We began the day by going to McDonald's for breakfast and then to the grocery store to get a few items for the weekend. We headed home to do some work outside.

We enjoyed hanging out together, father and son.

Then it happened. Right before my eyes. One moment he was acting like a normal five-year-old boy and enjoying what little boys like to do. The next moment he was whining and yelling at me and making no logical sense at all. I stood there watching my son, seriously wondering who had just taken over his body. I was thinking, *Really? Is this the way you're going to act? You're about to mess up a really good day!*

Most days when he acts this way, I get pulled into the fray, and I end up asking myself why I am arguing with this little minion. But for some reason this morning God graced me with some insight.

I remembered some things I had learned about brain chemistry. This outlandish behavior of my child probably wasn't an alien takeover but simply a nutrition and/or hydration issue. His brain had slipped into survival mode because he needed food and water.

Most of us, when we feel a little run down or even grouchy we have the thought, *I should eat a snack*. And if we have learned anything about nutrition, we will grab something that will help our blood sugar regulate which in turn will help us act better.

But sometimes we need someone else to help us out with this.

On that sunny February day, my son needed me to help him out. *I* needed to help him out. Mind you I didn't hand him a Snickers bar like you see in commercials, even though he would have loved that. But I did get him something a tad bit healthier to eat and some water. Even though it took some time, he did finally regulate back into an enjoyable little dude without too much anguish on my part.

Many times our kids come to us severely malnourished. The malnourishment obviously affects their physicality, but it also damages their brain chemistry.

Let's return to Carie and Kirby's two foster daughters. This is how they described them the first time they met:

"They couldn't walk much at all. The two-year-old would fall almost every three to four steps. She had bald patches on her head of curls, and her hair was incredibly dry. You could barely understand her when she spoke, so it was a guessing game the majority of the day to understand her wants and needs. The three-year-old had stringy, brittle hair that almost looked grey. She was incredibly skinny and frail. Her ribs were showing and her arms and legs were so petite. She always had a blank look on her face and her eyes were glassed over."

These girls had classic cases of malnourishment.

What happened next I am sure many of you have had happen in your own homes:

"The two-year-old girl did not seem quite as under-nourished (besides the bald patches on her head and dry hair) as the three-year-old, but she hoarded food. Sometimes we found her in the pantry with the door closed eating. When we would catch her, she looked at us with eyes as big as saucers."

"She snuck food in her room. We found food in odd places—under blankets, under the bed, in the closet, in the toys. Why would a two-year-old hoard food? Was she worried about when she might get food again? Worried she wouldn't get enough food? Those were questions that went through my mind. So we moved up snack times and ate more frequently to reassure her."

If we want to empower our children to make good choices, we have to get in tune with their physiological needs.

My son didn't understand why he was melting down. Carie and Kirby's foster daughter didn't know why she was hoarding food. We could have tried all day to correct their poor behavior, and we would have failed. Their behavior wasn't even their fault.

What would we have accomplished if we corrected their behavior or even punished them for it? Correction or punishment would have pushed them further into survival mode. Now they would be fighting for food and water along with protecting themselves. Not much correcting gets done when that is happening.

Instead after I got my son some water and a snack and he calmed down, we sat down, and then I addressed his behavior—not for the sake of punishment but so that he could learn a better way to communicate with me what he needed.

For children like Carie and Kirby's it takes even longer because that young child needed to "feel" like she had enough to eat.

Part of the teaching moment in either of these cases is to help our children know that they have a voice. We can teach them how to communicate to others to get what they need in ways that do not include tantrums or bizarre behaviors like hoarding food in the bedroom.

How well does your child use his or her voice? Do they scream and demand that their needs get met? Do they manipulate or control their environment? Or do you have a child that never speaks up at all?

How to give a child a voice can be a little confusing. We don't want to create a monster who argues with us on every little thing. In this next chapter, I explain what giving your child a voice means, why it is important to give your child a voice, and how you can give your child a voice.

CHAPTER ELEVEN

Giving Your Child a Voice

My son wakes up early. If he senses any daylight, he wakes up—hollering or yelling. If we are lucky he wakes up just talking—non-stop.

I remember one day when he was just beginning to say a few words. One of Danielle's friends was over at the house, and my son began expressing very loudly what he wanted. Our friend smiled and said, "He is finding his voice."

I glanced at her with a puzzled look. I wasn't sure what she meant.

What Does It Mean to Give a Child a Voice?

It is common for a child that comes to us from foster care or through adoption to not have a voice regardless of their age.

Babies that get no response to their cries learn to not cry anymore. Even a toddler learns to meet their own needs as best they can, doing things that no one would expect a child that age to do, such as feeding themselves or getting themselves in bed. Teenagers revert to manipulation as they try to get their needs met.

All are examples of a child with no voice. A baby stops crying because when they cry, no one comes. A toddler stops asking a parent or caretaker for basic needs because when they did, no one took care of them. A teenager uses manipulation because when they used their voice, no one cared.

One of the powerful ways we as parents can empower and help our children feel safe and heal from trauma is to give them a voice.

Our son was, as you know by now, eight months old when CPS placed him with us. Like any baby, he cried, screamed, and yelled when he was hungry, wet, alone, or afraid. We immediately responded, even if it was over and over.

He definitely used his voice. That tells me that at least someone responded to him before he came to us.

If you adopted a child that spent time in an orphanage, you might have noticed he or she doesn't cry much, maybe not at all. You can find many stories of people shocked by how quiet a room full of babies is in many orphanages. We expect to hear crying, even wailing, when we enter a room full of babies.

But what happens when no one responds to a baby's cry? It doesn't take very long for that baby to stop crying.

We want to hear our babies cry.

Our son now talks from the moment he wakes up until he goes to bed. I am an introvert, and Danielle and I didn't have to share airspace with anyone in our home for over 20 years. So my first reaction many times is to ask him to be quiet. I know, just a little selfish on my part.

I tend to get offended when I don't have any room for my own voice, and I don't do a good job of fully listening to my son. Often he does this: "Hey Dad look at this," and then he looks at me to see if I am looking at him. If I am not, he says, "Dad, Dad, Dad—look at this!" So I look at him, and while he is telling me what he wants me to hear, he keeps glancing at me to see if I am still fully listening.

I have made note of this because it communicates to me that he doesn't feel that I hear him.

Why Having a Voice Is Important

I know for some cultures it is taught that children should be seen and not heard. That sounds nice to my selfish ears, but it certainly doesn't promote healthy, connected children. Nor does total chaotic kid anarchy either!

When I give my son a voice he learns that:

- **He is safe.** It's normal for things to frighten children. When I give my child the opportunity to talk about his fears, he is able to process what frightens him. He begins to feel safe, not only from the thing that frightens him but also in his vulnerable sharing with me.

- **It's okay to have needs and wants.** Needs and wants don't go away after we are a baby. We have them for the rest of our lives. The trouble is that many of us don't ever learn how to express these in healthy ways. When I let my son voice his needs and wants, he learns that it's okay to have them. He also learns that I am willing to listen to them. And when I can and it's appropriate, I want to help meet them.

- **He doesn't have to demand.** The more voice I give him and the better I listen, the less my son tries to control, manipulate, or triangulate in order to be heard. He also gets angry much less often resulting in fewer tantrums and meltdowns.

How Can I Give a Voice to My Child?

First, I have to understand the importance of giving my son a voice and how that helps us connect. Honestly, I need reminding of that truth often.

Second, I need to remember that I am an adult with years of experience and that my son is experiencing many things for the first time. He needs to express. And I need to **learn to listen.**

I probably even need to learn how to hear my son's distinct voice. What does that tone, that cry, and that laugh mean?

Physically and emotionally I can give my son a voice by stopping what I am doing, when I can, looking him in his eyes, even lightly touching him on his arm or cheek, and listening to him. This takes me being fully present with him.

When I am able to give my son his voice, he feels valued, loved, and connected. That is empowering. And when I need to correct him, he is more likely to receive the correction.

Empowering our child by giving him or her a voice can intimidate any parent. What if they have questions I don't want or know how to answer? What about thoughts that I am uncomfortable discussing? And what in the world do I do with emotions?

One way I can give my son a voice is by helping him express his emotions. And chances are any child from a hard place will have HUGE emotions. It's important for us as parents to learn how to help our children express their big emotions. Read on as I not only share from my experience but also from an expert on the topic.

CHAPTER TWELVE

Helping Your Child Express Emotion

> *"Remember that emotion is not a debatable phenomenon. It is an authentic reflection of our subjective experience, one that is best served by attending to it."*
> —*Curt Thompson,* **Anatomy of the Soul: Surprising Connections Between Neuroscience and Spiritual Practices That Can Transform Your Life and Relationships**

The first few years of our marriage I didn't attune well to my wife's emotions—especially when she got excited about something. As an expressive person, she jumped, laughed, ran around, and screamed with excitement—all while I stood with a simple smile on my face and would say, "That's great honey."

That response, or lack thereof, always threw a wet blanket on her excitement. I definitely wasn't attuned to her emotions.

Then we got a little guy who also has big emotions. Some of this is his personality no doubt. But most kids from a hard place come to us with big emotions. They are trying to make sense of everything that has happened to them.

Even though I learned a lot about meeting someone in the midst of their emotion from my wife, I still struggle with big emotions—mine or any other person's. It shows as I interact with my son. My default response is either frustration or shutting down. Unfortunately that communicates to my son that his feelings lack value and maybe even are wrong to have. Both cause shame.

The last thing I want to do is shame my son for having emotion just because *I* don't know how to deal with emotion. But I know it happens. I come from the generation of "big boys don't cry."

When We Encourage Proper Expression of Emotion

The key is to first accept that emotion is a part of the human experience. It's how we are created. Our kids that come to us with traumatic histories need to know it's okay for them to have emotion—even BIG emotion.

The challenge is when our children struggle with how to express their emotions in ways that don't cause harm to others. But if they are never allowed or encouraged to process these emotions, they will never learn.

When we empower our kids to express their emotions in safe ways, a lot of positive things happen:

- **Acceptance.** Our kids feel accepted especially when they have emotions that they don't know how to handle. We all know how it feels when an emotion hijacks us. Something out of nowhere triggers an emotional response, and we can't stop it even if we try. Acceptance gives our children a safe place to emote.

- **Honor.** Our culture seems to have lost its ability to honor. Maybe that stems from a lack of honor in our families. When we allow our kids to be who they are without judgment, we show them respect. That is a form of honor.

- **Attunement.** When I am attuned to my son's emotions, we are in harmony. I can show that I am attuned to my son's emotions by full-body listening. My facial expressions support, maybe even mirror, his emotions. If he is jumping up and down excited, I jump up and down with excitement. If he is crying because a friend hurt his feelings, then my voice and face join him in his sadness.

> *"When a child is upset, logic often won't work until we have responded to the right brain's emotional needs. We call this emotional connection 'attunement', which is how we connect deeply with another person and allow them to 'feel felt'. When parent and child are tuned in to each other, they experience a sense of joining together."*
> — Dr. Dan Siegel, The Whole Brain Child

Sometimes this can backfire because my son doesn't think I am authentic in my emotional response. It comes across as if I am making fun of him. So I try to temper my response while still meeting him within his big emotion. Maybe if my action overshadows his, it takes the focus away from him and puts it on me.

What I am learning is how to help my son understand what emotions are, how to communicate them appropriately, and that they are temporary.

In *The Whole Brain Child*, Dr. Dan Siegel shares a helpful tool that helps our children navigate, or SIFT through, their emotions. (I wish I had learned this as a young child.)

- **Sensations**

Emotion is so much more than anger or happiness. Those feelings or sensations are usually easy to identify in a child's body. If my son feels like hitting someone and his fists are clenched, odds are he knows he is angry. If he is smiling and jumping around a bit because I offered him some ice cream, I would say he knows he is happy.

But what about that uneasy feeling in his stomach, or when his shoulders feel heavy, or his eyes want to fixate on the floor? What do these sensations mean?

Simple awareness of these emotions will help our children learn how to both communicate and respond appropriately.

- **Images**

Our son, like many children, awakes often from dreams or nightmares. He doesn't usually tell us what they are, but often fear is associated. I need to ask him if he can remember any images from his dreams.

Even though our son was eight months old when he was placed with us, I think he remembers things from an early age. Often he will tell us about things he remembers, both good and bad. These are lasting images in his brain.

Strong emotions are attached to images. We as parents can prevent these images from having a fearful power over our children.

- **Feelings**

We can help our children sift through their feelings and specifically identify them rather than give vague descriptions like "I'm fine" or "I'm sad." Some friends of mine took a chart of faces describing different emotions and made placemats out of them. They have four boys, and it's fun to hear them tell stories about dinnertime at their house. It was a common practice to go around the table and have each person use the placemat to identify three emotions they had felt that day. I love it!

We can help our children identify specific feelings like "anxious," "disappointed," or "excited."

- **Thoughts**

If we can help our children capture the emotional thoughts going through their mind, then we can talk through them. This helps a child transition from a big emotional response triggered by the survival part of their brain to a more calming thinking response to their emotions.

What Makes This Challenging

Understanding that our child needs to express their emotions and knowing how to help them navigate those emotions are only part of the battle. If I don't know how to do this myself, I can't help my son very well. It's not uncommon that we as adults don't know how to express our own emotions. I really didn't know I had many emotions until well into my 20s. I thought I was either happy, sad, or angry. That's it. And I sure didn't talk to people about my emotions.

If that describes you, I encourage you to learn how to express your own emotions in healthy ways. You don't have to do this before you can help your child. You can even help each other master expressing your emotions.

Please don't ignore this. One of the best ways you can connect and empower your child toward healing is to model healthy expressing of your own emotions.

We have processed a lot so far. How are you doing? I hope the vulnerable stories you read here help you when you feel that maybe you blow it a lot as you try to apply parenting with connection principles.

I don't think it was a mistake that your child is in your family. I believe that you have what they need and that you can help them heal.

If you feel defeated or you lack hope that things will get better with your child, please take a moment to allow that last sentence to sink in. I do really believe you have what it takes to parent your child.

Encouragement and praise build us up, help us feel better about ourselves, and give us hope. In the next chapter, I share with you seven things that your child needs to hear from you.

CHAPTER THIRTEEN

Your Child Needs Your Encouragement and Praise

You might have noticed that I have referenced a few times about how we can subtly shame our kids. The sad thing is that a kid that comes from a hard place innately feels shame. Anyone who experiences loss, trauma, neglect, or abuse will feel shame. What I mean is that they will feel that something is intrinsically wrong with who they are.

I don't think we as parents understand, or at least we forget, how delicate a child's heart is. I wrote a blog post, "15 Ways We Shame Our Children (www.kennethacamp.com/15Ways)," in which I talk about one way that we shame our children is by withholding praise.

Praise and encouragement are like free currency that we can lavishly invest into our child's emotional bank.

As parents wanting to connect with our children that come to us from foster care or adoption, this is an easy win. Yet if you are like me, I tend to point out what my son is doing wrong way more often than I encourage him or praise him for things.

It's easy for me to see what happens within my very expressive son when I correct his poor behavior over and over. His eyes drop to the floor, and his shoulders slump. He turns away from me. Or his eyes flame with anger. His fists clench. His stance hardens. And hateful words fly.

These and similar reactions to not only withholding encouragement and praise but also over-correcting cause our children to think something is wrong with them. That is toxic shame.

When I do offer my son encouragement and praise, as you can imagine—and I hope you also see this in your child—his body language communicates confidence, pleasure, relief, joy, and, yes, connection. His eyes light up. He looks into my face, even for just a second. He turns toward me. Many times he even snuggles close into me.

I can tell the days when I am doing better at this because my son will randomly say, "Hey Dad?" "Yes son?" "I love you Dad."

Most times he says this almost in a whisper and many times while he is busy playing or working on something. That's okay with me. In that sweet moment, I know our hearts are connected.

Things to Remember

- It's easy to respond to negative behaviors. We have plenty of opportunities to correct our children. Dr. John Gottman[ii], a renowned couple therapy expert, coined the phrase the "Magic Ratio." He states that healthy couples have a ratio of five positive comments to one another for every negative comment. This ratio holds true for other relationships too, such as the parent—child relationship.

- Encourage and praise a lot. Don't be afraid that you will over do it. You *can't* overdo it.

- Intentionally look for opportunities. If you have a kid who is really acting out, this might be difficult, but that makes it even more important.

- Don't wait for a good result or behavior. Praise your child for a good effort even if the result turns out to be not so good. Also, randomly point out qualities or characteristics about your child that you like or appreciate.

7 Things Your Child Needs to Hear You Say

Remember that your words are powerful. They can either build up or tear down. Whether a foster or adopted child is a few hours old or in their teens when placed in your home, they need the transforming power of edifying words spoken into their lives.

1. **You are safe.** Trauma puts a child on high alert. Many times we label them as hyperactive when they are really hyper-vigilant. They can't let their guard down, and they are constantly observing their environment looking for danger. They can never hear too often from us that they are now safe.

2. **You can act your age.** Not "Why can't you act your age?" Especially children who have spent some years in foster or institutional care have lost their ability to just play. They probably had to make too many decisions, take care of younger siblings, or protect themselves. This robs them of their childhood. They need to gently hear over and over that it's okay to be a child.

3. **Yes.** Remember chapter 7? I far too often default to "No". Sometimes it's "No, no, NO!" I consciously look for opportunities to say yes. Many times I stop myself when about to say no and ask myself if it's possible at all to say yes.

4. **You matter.** The deepest wound is neglect. A child that no one notices and is rejected or abandoned struggles with self-worth.

5. **I notice you.** You are seen and heard. Of course we notice them when they misbehave. Often a child from a hard place misbehaves for many other

reasons other than rebellion. What about when they act as we want them to act? Our children need random, unsolicited words of praise and delight.

6. **You belong.** Every child needs a sense of belonging. In my conversations with people who aged out of the foster care system, one of the most powerful sources of healing for them was knowing that they had a place of belonging. Even if a child is in our homes for a matter of days, we can speak this into their lives. We don't need to withhold out of a fear of experiencing our own feeling of loss.

7. **You are loved.** Of course every child needs to know they are loved. A child from a hard place may pull away from touch, but you can always express proper words of affection. Yes, sometimes we need help in feeling affection for a difficult child. Yet if we want to help that child heal, we need to communicate to them often and in many ways that they are loved.

These past four chapters about Transitions, Sleep and Nutrition, Voice, and Encouragement are simple ways to empower your kid. The common denominator is how well we play the detective. If we do it well, we will notice what our child needs to give him or her the best opportunity to succeed.

Another need that often goes unnoticed is a child's sensory processing challenge. Sensory processing disorders affect many kids, not just those who come from a hard place. Yet far too often these kids get mislabeled as troublemakers.

Let's take a little refresher about sensory processing in the next chapter. I also have a treat for you that you don't want to miss. It is a link to a podcast with a therapist who works with sensory processing disorders. Her insight is invaluable.

CHAPTER FOURTEEN

Helping Your Child Process Sensory Input

I sat at a table just outside the door to the playroom at Chick-Fil-A while my son played inside. I occasionally looked up to make sure he was doing okay then I would return to reading.

I looked up again to see, to my astonishment, my son standing on a bench inside the playroom licking the window like he was one of those sucker fish that clean the inside of an aquarium. He licked the window back and forth in long, wet, sloppy strokes.

When I jumped up out of my seat, I saw two couples sitting at a table exactly on the other side of the window. All four stared at my son with their mouths gaping. They didn't really have a look of disgust. It was more a look of "Why do I keep staring at this?"

I walked in and tried to calmly peel my son off the window as I mouthed to his admirers, "I am SORRY!" Then we quietly and quickly slipped out of the restaurant.

Sensory Processing

Until we began fostering I knew nothing about sensory processing. Sensory processing is how the brain receives and organizes information. Of course, we do that through our senses of sound, taste, touch, sight, and smell.

In relation to parenting with connection, as with many things, one of the first steps is to understand that your child's unexplainable, even crazy behavior most likely isn't because he or she wants to act poorly. No, they don't want to anger you, embarrass you, or defy your authority.

Simply, if they struggle with processing sensory input, they probably don't even notice you, much less hear you. At the very least, their response to you is delayed because of it.

I have learned to not overreact to my son when he licks odd surfaces, including the top of my bald head. Or when he struggles with where his body is in relation to others, often banging his body into them. Other times his voice gets louder and louder drowning out even my own thinking. Or when he gets obsessed with touching something because he *has* to find out what it feels like before he can do anything or listen to anyone.

When my son was four he attended a Vacation Bible School where they learned some songs during the week. He knew all the songs by heart and would sing them around the house. I enjoyed hearing his sweet voice singing these songs.

At the end of the week, the teachers lined up all the kids on the stage on risers. The room had glaring lights. The music was upbeat and turned up loud. They placed my son on the top row, right in the middle. I thought to myself, *He has no escape route or adult close enough to keep him calm.*

Sure enough, by the second song, he was climbing on and shaking the back of the risers. Then he jumped back down and began talking loudly a few inches from his friend's face.

Danielle and I sat in our seats, not horrified but painfully sad because we understood what was happening—sensory overload.

If my goal was to control or modify his behavior, I would have scolded his behavior. Please understand that his behavior wasn't acceptable, but it wasn't rebellious either.

However, if I parent with the goal of connecting with my child, I work on responding to my child's needs. I educate myself on his behaviors so that I can understand how his brain receives and organizes the world around him. And I work with and for him to help him interact with his environment.

That empowers him for success.

Everyone Has to Process Sensory Input

It helps to remember that we all process through our senses. And even as adults many of us struggle with processing sensory input.

I struggle with processing audio input like crowded, noisy rooms. I used to think that my struggle was a personality thing. Then I learned that it was a sensory issue. Someone could easily interpret my behavior as non-social, introverted, and maybe even arrogant. But in reality, I withdraw, stand quietly in the corner, or even leave the room simply because I can't handle the sensory input.

Now before you shake your head at how strange that sounds, think about how you process sensory input. What situations cause you to feel anxious or out of control? Or what do you do to help you concentrate on a task?

Do you sometimes overreact to a situation and later wonder why you did that? Ever think that you simply had trouble with processing the sensory input?

How can you tell what is the cause of your child's (or anyone's child) action? First of all, please don't blame yourself if your child suffers from sensory processing challenges. Many different things can attribute to a child's struggles with sensory processing. If a child has experienced any kind of trauma, especially from pre-natal to one year old, that's a likely cause. But it can also simply be genetic or environmental.

The first thing to do is to correctly identify your child's action so that you have the appropriate response. If your child's actions are caused by trouble processing their sensory world and you attempt to correct "bad" behavior, well let's just say you won't have much success.

Want to dig a little deeper into this subject? I recorded this interview with Marti Smith. Marti is certified in Therapeutic Listening, Interactive Metronome, CiSM, Athletic Training, and Massage Therapy. She enjoys gathering information and helping other therapists organize it into practical and useful resources. Her desire to help others comes out loud and clear in this interview. Listen in to our conversation here at www.kennethacamp.com/session8.

Here are a few nuggets I picked up from Marti:

- Everyone has sensory processing challenges. The question is how does it impact your day to day activities.

- Some have hypo sensory processing. Others have hyper sensory processing. Do you know the difference and which your child has?

- A parent needs to know their own child to know whether or not they need help with sensory processing issues.

- You can understand how to parent better if you do understand your child's sensory input needs.

Here are some resources that also might help:

- Sensory Processing Disorder Foundation website - www.spdstar.org/basic/about-spd

- Creative Therapies with Marti Smith - www.creativetherapies.com

- *The Out-of-Sync Child Has Fun, Revised Edition: Activities for Kids with Sensory Processing Disorder,* Revised Edition

For more resources for sensory processing help go to the Resource section of the book.

So we have been talking a lot about connecting and empowering our kids, but when and how do we correct them? Remember Parenting with Connection is never a permissive parenting approach. The key is learning how to correct while still empowering and connecting with your child. In the next few chapters, I will help you figure out ways to do just that.

CORRECTION

"When we shift our perspective from the outward to the inward, from rules to relationships, our parenting will change."
—*Leslie Fields*, **Parenting Is Your Highest Calling and Eight Other Myths that Trap Us in Worry and Guilt.**

CHAPTER FIFTEEN

Responding Appropriately to Your Child

Here is my constant inner battle: I want my child to obey me—immediately. And I want to stay connected to my child. If my need for compliance wins the battle, I react to his poor behavior more like a monarch ruling my little kingdom. My child is my loyal—he better be anyway—subject. And when he fails to follow my mandates, punishment follows.

But wait a moment. That's not how I really want to parent, at least not long term. You don't either or you wouldn't be reading this book.

We want to parent our children with compassion, responding to them with value and honor. Yes we want them to make good choices and follow our instructions, but not as a subject would a ruler. Instead we want obedience flowing out of trust and connection.

Okay, let's get real for a minute. All that is easy to say, and we all nod our head in agreement. In a perfect world that is how we parent. And those are the moments we capture and post on Facebook or put in our end-of-the-year newsletter. You know exactly what I mean.

But what about those ugly parenting incidents? Thank goodness those aren't captured on video.

Here is how I overreacted just the other day. Our night-time routine consists of dinner, an after-dinner treat, play time, bath time, an after-bath snack, brushing teeth, going to the bathroom, reading books, then (big sigh) finally snuggles and prayer time in bed.

This night Danielle was out running errands. I had been up since 5 am and had spent most of the day working on the rough draft of this book. My brain was mush. I was tired. My son was tired too—the perfect ingredients for an explosive bath time.

Before getting into the bathtub, my son completely missed the toilet while peeing. He peed all over the floor because he was too busy talking to me instead of paying attention. I yelled, "Look where you are peeing!" and I picked him up and put him in the bathtub.

I muttered and sighed as I cleaned up the floor then stormed out of the bathroom. I returned to help him bathe, get out, dry off, then make our way to the kitchen for his after-bath snack. I dutifully gave him a couple of choices, but he couldn't make up his mind probably because he either wasn't hungry or didn't like his choices.

Already in a bad mood over the bathroom incident, I hollered at him again, "Can you please make up your mind." Now he was hollering back at me.

Yeah, we were *both* in meltdown mode. I will spare you the rest of the drama, but let's just say it got worse before it got better.

The point is that I didn't respond appropriately.

Let's refresh our memory on some connected parenting tools that should help us respond appropriately to our kids.

Ways to Respond Appropriately

Take an IDEAL approach.[iii]

- **Immediate**—Brain research shows that if we respond within three seconds to our child's behavior (good or bad), he or she learns.

- **Direct**—Get within arms length and be fully present rather than distracted or hollering across the room with orders.

- **Efficient**—This refers to the levels of response below. Match the level of engagement or response rather than overreacting.

- **Action Based**—Give your child body memory for doing the right things to override the body memory of the wrong things. For example, give your child a "re-do." (We will look at this further in the next chapter)

- **Level**—Level your correction at the behavior, not the child.

Dr. Purvis shares three goals with the IDEAL approach:

1. Behavior is changed.

2. Parent and child are more connected.

3. Both are content because they succeeded.

In the video clip you can link to below, Dr. Karyn Purvis describes our response to our children's poor behavior as sometimes like going after a fly with a shotgun. She practically teaches how to respond appropriately:

- **Playful Engagement.** Respond with playful engagement for mild behavior by maybe asking them, "Are you asking or telling me?"

- **Structured Engagement.** If the child defiantly responds with something like, "I'm telling!" firmly respond with something like, "Okay, I'm giving you two choices: clean up you room now or after dinner."

- **Calming Engagement.** Sometimes that doesn't work, and the child escalates their behavior. Instead of allowing that to create utter chaos, use something like offering them a compromise. As Dr. Purvis says, this sounds counterintuitive. But if you remember in chapter 10, we talked about giving our kids a voice. This does that!

- **Protecting Engagement.** Sometimes, and this should be in rare cases, we need to engage our kid in a protective way, such as holding them, so they don't cause harm to themselves or others by acting out aggressively.

Watch this video clip – www.kennethacamp.com/IDEAL by Dr. Karyn Purvis as she goes into more depth on the IDEAL approach and the different levels of engagement.

The tools mentioned—re-dos, choices, and compromises—are covered in more depth in the next couple of chapters.

Let's review my response to the "peeing on the floor" incident.

I am laying myself out here to talk through how I could have responded more appropriately when my son peed all over the floor.

The fact that I was physically and mentally tired wasn't going to change. Extending grace is needed in times like this—grace both for myself and for my son. Maybe I could have communicated to him before we began bath time that I was very tired, so I needed his help.

Still, the exact same scene most likely would have happened. It's easy to see that things went downhill when I reacted by yelling at my son for peeing on the floor (for the 100th time). Sure my reaction was immediate, and I was direct, fully present, and within arms' length.

But my reaction lacked efficiency. My reaction was way overblown and didn't match my son's behavior.

Since my response broke down at the efficiency level, we didn't have a chance for positive body memory. I will explain body memory in more depth in the next chapter, "Offering Your Child a Re-Do."

Results I Look for by Responding Appropriately

When my child responds to me with things like a poor attitude, defiance, or complete disobedience, I want to respond in a way that accomplishes more than total dominance. I assure you that I have failed as much as I have succeeded in how I respond. However, when I succeed I see results that encourage me to keep working at it.

- **Remain engaged.** I want a healthy connection with my son. I want him to trust me for what he needs, and I hope that leads to a healthy relationship well into adulthood.

- **Help him put the lid back on.** When my son has a meltdown, it's like he flips his lid. He is no longer using the complex part of his brain. Instead he is using the lower, survival mode. My response can help my son shift from his out-of-control emotional state and back into a balanced emotional state.

- **Help them get it right.** Any child, but especially one with a trauma affected-brain, needs someone to come alongside and help them get it right. What I mean is to learn how to navigate their big feelings, to learn how to communicate what they feel and need, and to learn how to do it well.

- **Honor.** In all of this, I hope to develop a culture of honor in our home. When that is a core value, it drives many things, such as how I respond to my son. I want him to grow up knowing that he has value and purpose. I want him to know that even though he experienced loss as a young child that doesn't define who he is.

When I respond appropriately to him, I avoid casting more shame onto his soul. Rather I can help heal the broken places where shame tends to creep in. For example, "Why didn't my birth family try harder to keep me? Is there something wrong with me?" He hasn't asked me that question as of yet, but his actions sometimes do ask that very thing.

I have a choice in the way I respond to my son. I can work at responding appropriately which will communicate honor and value, or I can respond poorly and deepen the shame he feels about himself.

Are you ready to look a little deeper at one of the tools Dr. Purvis recommended in the IDEAL approach? Lets' take a look at how to apply "re-dos" in this next chapter. We get to see how I respond to my son when he swung the TV remote around his head and let it fly across the room after I asked him to hand it to me. I am sure it will give you hope.

CHAPTER SIXTEEN

Offering Your Child a Re-Do

Before learning Parenting with Connection principles, I didn't understand the purpose of this parenting tool. I'm not really sure I saw it applied often. But when I think about how I want to disciple my son, to help him learn how to make good choices rather than poor ones, it makes a lot of sense.

I will get into how it makes more sense, but first, here is a story that happened recently when I did a decent job of applying this correcting principle. Honestly, I could choose from hundreds of stories to illustrate this one.

One day after my son watched his afternoon TV show, I asked him to hand me the remote. The remote has a strap handle on it that he likes to use to swing it around his head. I have told him many times that is not what the strap is for.

But once again he swung it around and around his head as he walked over to me. I am not sure how he thought he would hand the remote to me, but he didn't quite make it to me when it flew out of his hand and past my head and crashed to the ground behind me.

The battery cover and batteries ricocheted all over our tile floor. We stared at each other in a moment of silence that seemed like an hour.

I will return to that in a moment. I did offer him a "re-do" by the way.

I like using "re-dos" as a way of correcting and use it a lot. The way I see it, no one is keeping score on how many times we get it wrong—at least they shouldn't be. When my son talks to me inappropriately, makes a poor choice with his actions, or any other misbehavior, I often give him an opportunity to try it again.

This way of correcting works if you can catch the misbehavior before it escalates which can't always happen. The key is to stay calm and prevent escalation.

I observe preschool and elementary teachers do this well. At the beginning of a school year, the kids make all kinds of poor choices. Take for instance the first few days when it's time for the class to line up to go to recess. Kids push, cut in line, complain, shout, and maybe even run out of the room. A well-trained teacher patiently shows the class how to get in line the correct way. They might even practice it a few times. In a matter of a few days that same class of rowdies is seen lining up with their hands to themselves then walking in an orderly fashion through the hallways on their way to recess.

We can help our own kids learn the same way by getting them to do it over the correct way when they do something wrong.

So the remote is lying on the floor with its batteries strewn everywhere. This time I say, "Wow dude. I don't think that was the way we want do that. I asked you to hand the remote to me. Let's try that again. I will help you pick up the batteries and remote, and then I want you to hand it to me, okay?"

The key is for him to physically do the action the right way. I don't do it for him. I don't let him off the hook by saying, "Next time I want you to do it the right way." Even if he resists, I stand firm until he puts the remote in my hand.

Why is this so important? I want him to create a physical, not just a mental, memory of himself doing the right thing. The more he does this, the more this "feels right" for him.

As an athlete, I learned the principle of body memory many years ago. This is why a basketball player will shoot hundreds of jump shots or a baseball player will field endless numbers of grounders. The focus is on practicing the correct form and doing it right. The more our bodies make the correct motion, the more our bodies remember it. It becomes second nature. If my jump shot isn't going in during a game, I return to the basics of the motion to reinforce the body memory.

That is exactly what we are doing when we give our kids a re-do. "That wasn't the result we want, so let's work on the right way and do it again"

If my objective is to train or disciple my child in healthy ways to handle emotions, navigate conflict, and relate to others well, then this works great.

Again, offering a "re-do" works well in response to mild behavior, especially when you engage your child playfully. You are staying connected by avoiding a survival response, you are empowering by giving them a chance to reinforce positive body memory, and you corrected their poor behavior. Great job!

But we all know that our kids don't always respond to that level of engagement. You might even have one that never does, but I would still begin there. However, when they escalate, that is when we move to giving them choices and offering them compromises.

I struggle sometimes with how to do these well while still feeling like I am in control. Stay with me as I explain what I mean.

CHAPTER SEVENTEEN

Giving Your Child Choices and Offering Them Compromises

If I as a parent have control issues, I will struggle to share power with my child.

Giving choices to our kids isn't about letting them choose what they want for dinner, although even that's okay, I guess. I used to think that my kid could eat what we were eating. And if we were at a restaurant, I would pick out my son's meal when he was four years old. I have softened on that a bit, but I still usually just give two or maybe three choices.

Here we are talking about when your child escalates their behavior and they don't respond to your offering of a re-do.

Going through this progression takes commitment to the process. Because if you are like me, I feel many times that I am being very lenient when I offer him a chance to try it again. If he keeps misbehaving, well, he had his chance; now it's time to lower the boom.

Maybe not that drastic, but that thought definitely goes through my mind.

More to It Than Giving Choices

Giving choices isn't just about "Do you want this or that for dinner?" Giving choices also empowers our kids to make good choices as a way of correcting.

My son acts impulsively and grabs toys from other kids. This gives me an opportunity (yay!) to empower him to make things right. So first I playfully say to him, "Hey, buddy, we don't grab toys from our friends. Let's try that again and use our words to ask for the toy."

Being the strong-willed boy he is, I often get the response, "No! I want to play with this toy. I found it first!"

If I do it well, I get close to him, bend down to eye level and say, "Son, we don't grab toys away from our friends. Now, do you want to give it back to Johnny, or do you want me to give it to him?"

I gave him two choices that I like. If I am still on my game, I patiently wait for him to decide which action he wants to take. I have corrected his behavior, shared some power with him, and avoided shaming him, and we stayed connected. That's a win—win.

I have not always been so patient. I usually can start off well, but when he stammers around or defiantly tells me no to both choices, I have been known to grab the toy from him, hand it back to his friend, and remove my son from the room (not always so gently).

I for sure correct him when that happens. But then I have a bigger mess on my hands. No doubt, he is in full meltdown mode. I am trying to regulate my emotions, and my attempt to empower backfires. And we are not even close to being connected.

When a Choice Is Really a Consequence

Sometimes when I think I am empowering my son, I am really correcting, no, threatening him with a consequence. I am not sharing my power as his dad with him, but rather I am attempting to control him with my words.

It sounds something like this: "You can either pick up your toys now or we won't get a treat after dinner." At first it sounds like a choice, but when you listen closely, I am telling him what he needs to do—or else.

A real sharing of power would be if I gave him two distinct choices that I am completely fine with him choosing either one. Maybe in the example above I am kind of okay if he chooses to forfeit the treat because he doesn't want to pick up his toys. But really, I want him to pick up his toys and I am trying to use a "choice" to get him to do what I want him to do.

What Giving Choices Does for Our Kids

Why is giving choices so important for our kids, especially those who come to us through foster care and adoption?

- **Voice.** I won't go into detail here, since I wrote about this in Chapter 11. Giving our kids opportunities to express their wants and needs empowers them. We want that to happen while they are young and in our care so that they have a strong safe-haven where they can try out their power.

- **Trust.** Trust is a two-way street. My son begins to trust me as I stick to honoring his choices (choices that I find acceptable), and he builds trust with me as he demonstrates his ability to voice his wants and follow through with his decision.

- **Honor.** Much like trust, as we learn to negotiate our wants and conflict well, we honor each other. I am big on creating a culture of honor in our home. At least that is my goal. I have a ways to go, but thankfully parenting is a fluid endeavor.

Offering Compromises

Have you heard these kinds of statements come from your kid? "No, I don't want either choice. I want to do it this way . . ." "I know how to do it." or harsher ones like "I will never do it your way! I hate you!"

I bet if you have, the hair stood up on the back of your neck. No parent, regardless of how they parent, should permit a child to talk to them in this manner. The difference is how we choose to respond.

Obviously, in this case the child's behavior escalated and is more aggressive. Whether you as a parent offer a compromise or not, definitely you need to become firmer. Still the objective is to stay connected. It's a little more challenging because he has or is close to flipping his lid.

So I offer him a compromise with the intent of keeping him engaged with me.

Again this might seem to threaten my authority as a parent, but I want my son to learn how to express his feelings and wants in a productive way. I want to teach him healthy conflict resolution. I don't want compliance when internally he feels anger or defeat.

Relational conflict happens when I instruct my son to do something and he wants to do something different. For example, I might tell my son that it is time to stop playing with his toys, brush his teeth, and put his shoes on. Even if I have been giving my son a five-, three-, one-minute countdown, he often isn't quite ready to stop playing, and he will ask me if he can play for a few more minutes.

I have a choice. I can bow up and respond, "No. I said that it's time to stop playing and brush your teeth and get your shoes on" Or I can offer a compromise. "Sure, I will let you play for one more minute, so go ahead and do one last thing."

What I want to avoid, because our little dude will try, is to let him keep asking for compromises. That isn't him learning how to resolve conflict. That is him trying to manipulate me.

Also, I stay in control of our schedule whenever we need to get out the door, or I want him in bed sooner rather than later.

Kids from a Hard Place Need Some Control

All of our kids benefit from us appropriately sharing our power with them, but children who have spent time in foster care or in an orphanage have had to be in control out of necessity and survival. If we suddenly grab that control away from them, we instantly push them into fear mode. No wonder they fight us on it.

Instead we can go into the relationship with eyes open to the need to negotiating new terms with them. This helps build trust, respect, and felt safety.

Learning this skill at a young age will help them their entire life. Think about it. You know adults who are terrible at expressing their wants or preferences. Instead of negotiating or working on a compromise, they demand, intimidate, and manipulate until they get what they want. Or they quit on the relationship.

When you look at offering compromises through this lens, it's easier to understand how this is a way we disciple them for successful relationships later in life too.

What happens when your kid gets more defiant and aggressive? I know you are familiar with Time Out but what about Time In? Join me in "Putting Your Child in Time In" so I can clarify the difference.

CHAPTER EIGHTEEN

Putting Your Child in Time In

This "level of engagement" stuff takes work. I do pretty good at it for awhile—well, for about 30 minutes—then my patience flies out the window.

I start thinking, *I don't know what your problem is, but I have about had enough with you.*

How quickly I forget. Uh, physical trauma, neglect, abandonment to name a few things are what his problem is.

My struggle is deciphering which behavior is trauma related and which is rebellious, defiant behavior. I know, it's next to impossible to tell which is which, and they get all mixed in together.

I now think that the levels of engagement are meant just as much for us parents as they are for the kids. I have to use my thinking brain: *Okay, respond with playful engagement. Well, that didn't work. Now give him two choices that I am okay with him choosing either one.*

That keeps me from flipping my lid. Usually.

That's why Time In works so well for *me*. Sometimes I need some time to regain my composure.

Seriously, why and when would we use Time In? If you are new to Parenting with Connection, you probably think I mean Time Out. No, this wasn't a missed typo. I meant to say Time In.

So what is the difference between Time In and Time Out?

The difference is simple really. When we put our child in Time In, we keep them close by, preferably in the same room. When we put our child in Time Out, we send them somewhere alone, usually their room.

The challenge with sending a child to Time Out, especially if they are out of control, is that they are forced to work things out on their own. If they tend to stuff their emotions, they never learn how to talk about their feelings.

If they are a child who yells and screams and says hurtful things and they are sent to their room, they are left to themselves to work out these big emotions. Yet they have no tools to do that.

In an attempt to correct behavior when we use Time Out, we create an environment that tends to feed fear-based responses. This can be true for any kid, but it is especially true for kids from a hard place.

Imagine if you had a history of abuse, neglect, or abandonment and you were sent to a room by yourself to "calm down and think about it."

It just won't happen. If you are using Time In or Time Out, your child has probably flipped their lid meaning they are using the emotional and fear-based part of their brain. Sending them to a place by themselves will only continue this response.

If they do calm down, they learn that no one is available or willing to help them navigate their big emotions. They learn that no one is safe.

With Time In, we keep our kids close by. Why is this important?

- **This helps him or her calm down.** My number one goal for Time In is to help my son regulate. Just moving to the spot I choose for him to sit begins the calming. If I am regulated, even hearing my breathing can help him calm down. What he needs in this moment is a healthy, regulated person close by that can help him calm himself.

- **It keeps parent and child engaged.** When we stay close, as in the same room, we can stay engaged. That might look like us making occasional eye contact. This works only if I am regulated! I can also say words of encouragement. If he is really struggling, I can sit down a few inches from him.

You mean we can talk when my child is in Time In? Of course. So often we use this tool as a way to punish, but that is not the goal at all. Our goal is always connection. If your child is in another part of the house and separated from you, connection will not happen.

- **Time In communicates that we are in it together**. This is especially important for a child that comes from a hard place. I want my son to know that I am here to help him navigate those feelings of anger, fear, confusion, abandonment, and so on. I want to walk with him through them, even while he is in the midst of them.

> *"Telling your child to calm down, or insisting they take time to themselves until they are calm can actually increase their internal distress. Instead, connection can calm the nervous system and keep feelings from getting too high."*
> —*Dr. Dan Siegel*

More Thoughts about Time In

Make sure it is warranted. I have used Time In in a knee-jerk fashion because I am so frustrated. When I do this, Time In is more punitive and a consequence than a tool to help my son regulate. And in those moments, it's usually an overreaction to his poor behavior.

Use an appropriate amount of time. I have read that the amount of time you give your child Time In is relative to your child's age. The norm is your child's age plus one minute. If your child is emotionally younger than their chronological age, then shorten the time. Obviously your child is not in Time In for a long time. Sometimes I need extra time to regulate myself, but I should be able to do that in a couple of minutes. If we send them away to another room for Time Out, it is easier to lose track of time.

Encourage use of words when reconnecting. As our children regulate, using words helps them move from the lower part of their brain to the more complex part of their brain. This helps them regulate even more. It helps them to possibly make sense of their big feelings and associated behavior (I need to make sense of it too!). We can also reassure them that we are okay, that we aren't going to leave them, and that we care about and love them.

Time In takes practice. Even as I write this chapter, I notice things I need to tweak about how I implement Time In. I still tend to use Time In as an angry reaction to my son's behavior. When I react out of anger and put him in Time In, I often am too harsh with him. I can also say things like "You just sit there until you can make a better choice." or "I don't want to hear a sound out of you." Because of my emotional reaction, I lose sight of the intended purpose of Time In which is to help my son regulate *his* emotional state. After that is accomplished we then can address his poor behavior.

Time In will look different depending on the age of your child. Sitting your five-year-old down in a chair in the living room for five minutes will work for them most of the time, but doing that with your 15-year-old probably won't accomplish what you want. I remember that the best thing for me as a 15-year-old was shooting baskets on the driveway with my dad. Yep. It helped me regulate and talk about things.

It took Danielle and I some time to learn how to implement Time In well. Go to www.kennethacamp.com/TimeIn and listen in on as we take a few minutes to discuss why we think Time In is important and how we finally began to do it well.

However you choose to use Time In with your kid remember it's not to punish them. Dr. Karyn Purvis taught three Cs to tell if you have done Time In well: Changed Behavior, Correction, and Contentment.

When Time In has that as the goal, it becomes a way for your child to feel safe and comforted rather than punished. I like that.

Sometimes as a parent we need to let our children know that if they keep making a poor choice, they will face a consequence. Find out in the next chapter how to handle consequences in a way that will get results. Also, it's important that we have good timing when we correct, so I will remove the mystery of timing too.

CHAPTER NINETEEN

Handling Consequences and Knowing When to Correct

My son loves going to Vacation Bible School. The church where he goes to VBS has a wrap up "Family Night" at the end of the week. It's like a big celebration—pizza, games, music, video presentation of the week, water slides, snow cones. My son lives for anything that resembles a party. As you can imagine, by the time we arrived at a recent Family Night, his body engine was on overdrive. I tried my best to prepare him for the behavior I expected.

He began the night great. He responded to me when I gave him boundaries. He kept checking in with me as he played outside with his friends. Then it was time to go inside for the presentation. Decorations all over the room. Dimmed lights. Loud music. People everywhere. Excitement filled the room.

My sensory processing challenged, precious son flipped out. He tried hard to stay regulated as I tried to give him loose boundaries. But when he began jumping on me, yelling in my face, and spitting at a friend who sat in the row behind us, I knew it was time to leave the room.

We went out into the lobby where it was quieter. I got him some water to drink as I worked to regulate both him and me.

He asked me, "Did we leave because it was a consequence for the way I was acting?" My heart sank. This communicated to me that he feels that I correct him often by using consequences.

I know it is a default way of parenting for me, but I don't use it efficiently most of the time. Usually I use it as an intimidation tool to get him to comply to my wishes.

Instead of handing out consequences as a first choice for correcting, this tool is best served as one of the last ones used. If not careful, the use of consequences, which are punitive in nature, can escalate the poor behavior, cause unwanted shame, and put the focus on the consequence rather than the correct behavior.

How to Use Consequences Well

Make sure to follow through. An easy pattern for parents to fall into is threatening a consequence in an attempt to get our child to stop doing something or to get them to do what we want them to do. When our child doesn't comply, rather than enforcing the consequence, which many times we never wanted or intended to enforce, we move to another tactic for compliance.

Each time we don't follow through, we lose the trust of our child. He or she needs to know that we mean what we say and that we will do it. This is true not only for discipline but also for every facet of your relationship. Your child might think, *If my dad won't follow through when he gives me a consequence, will he follow through when I need him?*

Understand the difference between natural and logical consequences. A natural consequence is what will naturally happen to a person if they continue the behavior. For example, if my son eats too much candy, he will feel sick to his stomach. Sometimes allowing natural consequences are healthy for our children because they learn cause and effect. However, of course, many times it's not safe, such as putting their hand in a fire or walking out into a busy street.

A logical consequence in this context is a parent led and enforced consequence.

Dr. Jane Nelson, author of *Positive Discipline*, teaches four Rs in relation to logical consequences:

- Related—Just as with a natural consequence, a logical consequence should relate to the misbehavior.

- Reasonable—Avoid a harsh, punitive tone to a consequence. The goal is to teach, not punish.

- Respectful—We can levy a consequence without shame, anger, or lectures.

- Revealed in Advance—This is where you can include your child in determining the consequence. This helps everyone to know what to expect, and it helps avoid overreaction.

That's a little different than my "You better do this or you will never get to go swimming again." Not very effective in so many ways. I think I will put this tool on the shelf as much as possible.

It's easy to think that I need to correct the behavior right when it happens. The trouble is that often when a child misbehaves, they are in an emotional state that limits or makes it impossible for them to even receive correction.

Earlier we talked about the IDEAL approach that Dr. Purvis taught. The "I" refers to Immediate. I often wrongly interpret that to mean that my correction needs to be immediate.

When Dr. Purvis teaches to respond immediately, this isn't always referring to correction. You as a parent need to put on your detective hat and determine if your child is able to respond to correction in that moment. You might need to immediately focus on connection and empowering. Then spend time on correcting at another time.

Dr. Purvis calls this practicing outside the moment.

So When Is It Best to Correct?

When your child is regulated. I have tried to correct my son when he is rolling around on the floor screaming. It just doesn't work. He is in full survival mode and isn't hearing a word I am saying. Any form of correction I try in this moment is a waste of my time and breath. I might as well work on helping him calm down instead.

What really gets me is how quickly he sometimes can go from all-out tantrums, calling me names, telling me he doesn't ever want to do A-N-Y-T-H-I-N-G with me again to "Daddy I love you." It makes me want to bang my head on the wall.

When your child is empowered. If I am focused on correcting my son when he is the midst of a meltdown or running around the restaurant like a whirling dervish yelling at the top of his lungs, I miss out on what he needs in that moment to help him regulate and calm down.

He needs me to figure out what he needs in that moment. Does he need to eat? Is he dehydrated? Does he need for me to notice him or listen to him? Is he on sensory overload? What will empower him so that he can begin self-regulating?

In most cases, until I figure this out, my attempt to correct him might just escalate the behavior. I have gone around that mountain so many times.

When you and your child are connected. Notice I said when "you *and* your child." That applies to when you both are regulated too. Effective parenting happens when we treat it like what it's meant to be—an intimate relationship.

If I help my child regulate and I empower him to make good choices, we will feel connected. We accomplished this together.

Now my child can receive my correction. We are both calmer. We can discuss solutions as a team. My child, especially as he or she gets older, takes more ownership in the correction.

Remember that the goal is not just behavior modification. It is to help our kids learn and grow. That is discipleship.

I hope this helps make these tools seem more real to you. If so, please join me here at my website, www.KennethACamp.com, so we can continue working together.

One more correcting tool that I think is easily overlooked is repairing our own mistakes. Really like many of these tools, this combines correcting with connecting and empowering. If you struggle with admitting when you are wrong, I can help you with that in the next chapter.

CHAPTER TWENTY

Repairing Your Mistakes

Unless you are a one-of-a-kind parent, you have made mistakes as you parent. You have lost your temper, yelled, threatened, and even spanked out of anger. You have grounded beyond reasonable logic, and you have regretted these mistakes.

I know you feel sometimes that you are the worst parent in the world, and you wonder if you should have brought this child into your home. You meant to help this child heal, to feel safe, and to have a family.

Before you completely cave in, STOP! You are not alone nor are you unique.

If no one else around you will honestly pull back the shades on their worst moments as a parent, I hope you have seen that I have in this book.

The thing about learning these parenting with connection principles from a book or class is that we hear the perfect scenarios: "Your child does this . . . you respond like this." You go through the prescribed steps, and it's magic. Your child behaves properly and loves you forever, singing your praises to the heavens.

Not quite.

Like anything, you don't really know how difficult something is until you try it for yourself.

Remember, Danielle and I didn't have children of our own. By the time CPS placed our son with us, we had enjoyed over 20 years of marriage. I say "enjoyed," but marriage is hard. We have had many good times, but we have had some very hard ones too.

One secret to a successful marriage is learning to repair your mistakes. Isn't any successful relationship like that?

You can imagine how clueless I was to how hard parenting can be. I witnessed it watching my siblings and friends, but until *you* are the parent, you just don't know.

The same is true for any parent who decides to foster or adopt. "How hard can this be? We have already raised three kids. We know what we are doing."

I can hear you laugh parent of a foster or adopted child. You know that it really isn't the same. A child from a hard place really does respond to you differently than your biological children.

Yes, parenting kids from a hard place is hard. Even if you have fostered many kids over the years, you know that not only are they different persons as we all are, but they each come to you with a different set of challenges.

When this is your reality, you will make mistakes. Perfect parenting isn't the goal. Intentional parenting is.

When we expect perfection from ourselves, it's near impossible to admit when we make mistakes. Words like "I am sorry and I was wrong" get stuck in our throats.

Accepting that you make a mistake with your child and then confessing it to them isn't a sign of weak parenting. Rather it will strengthen your relationship with your child. I promise.

So how can we repair our relationship with our children when we blow it?

Admit your wrong action and ask your child for forgiveness. Simple and straight to the point.

Here is an exercise from Empowered to Connect that will help:

Practice making mistakes with your child (not intentionally, of course) and repairing them so that you and your child can grow and learn, and your connection will strengthen. Choose a two-to-three day period when you will be with your child for most of the day. Over the course of these days, be mindful to repair each and every mistake you make when interacting with your child, whether you lose your temper, raise your voice, speak sarcastically, become frustrated, cut them off, fail to give them voice, ignore them, hurt their feeling, etc. Regardless of whether the mistake is big or small, intentional or unintentional, be sure to quickly, humbly, and sincerely repair each and every mistake you make.

As you do this, make a note of any observations that stand out, particularly in terms of your own feelings and your child's response (to both your mistake and your repair). Also make a note of any changes in your relationship with your child that you witness throughout the course of this time.

Any time I humbly admit to my young son that my actions were wrong and ask him to forgive me, he quickly responds with child-like sweetness, "Yes Daddy, I forgive you". Then he usually follows that with something like "You know Daddy, we don't yell in this house."

Yeah, buddy, you are right; we don't yell in this house. But more importantly whenever we do, we quickly make it right in this house.

Not only does this build trust and connection but it builds that culture of honor I seek for our home.

No matter how hard you try to get it right you *will* make mistakes. Believe it or not that's not all bad. While you certainly would never intentionally make mistakes with your child, being intentional to quickly repair your mistakes can make a tremendous difference for both you and your child. When you repair your mistakes quickly, humbly, and sincerely you are training your child because your action:

- **Models** right behavior and healthy ways of relating. It helps your child understand that *everyone* in the family "owns their stuff" and that you solve problems together.

- **Teaches** the importance of forgiveness and demonstrates how it should look. This helps your child learn the value of forgiveness and gives her practice seeking and giving it.

- **Promotes** healthy brain development which helps your child create new synaptic connections in the brain (in your brain too.)

I like this parenting with connection tool. I probably do this better than any of the others simply because I have had so much practice. I like it because it encompasses all three aspects of parenting with connection. When I ask my son to forgive me for blowing it, we almost always immediately connect. I definitely empower him as he now can choose whether to forgive me or not. And because of those two things, my son is much more open to correction in that moment.

It takes self-awareness in order to repair my mistakes. Some people are so narcissistic that they really don't think they make any mistakes. It's always the other persons fault that they act the way they do.

A successful parent will have a self-awareness knowing that in order to help their child heal, they need to know the way themselves. We, as parents, don't always know what to be aware of and if we do, what to do about it. In the last few chapters, I will help you figure that out.

SELF-AWARENESS

"You cannot lead a child to a place of healing if you do not know the way yourself."
—Dr. Karyn Purvis

CHAPTER TWENTY-ONE

Regulating Your Emotional State

Isn't it a shock when you see yourself on video? Often we say, "I didn't know I looked or sounded like that." We aren't aware of our tone, our posture, our facial expressions, or even how we communicate our emotions.

Part of self-awareness is recognizing that what we think or feel on the inside doesn't always translate accurately through our voice, emotions, and actions. Or do they?

Remember *Mister Rogers' Neighborhood*? I can hear him now singing his simple greeting song:

"It's a beautiful day in this neighborhood. It's a beautiful day for a neighbor. Could you be mine? Would you be mine?"

Hearing that song in my head calms me. He was always calm. Always smiling. Always pleasant.

How I wish I was more like that.

I remember when my son was about four years old, and I noticed him exploring my face when we talked or played, even when I corrected him. He still does this a lot. I think he is gauging to see how safe I am.

He looks to see how emotionally regulated I am. He notices my voice tone, volume, and cadence. He takes nonverbal cues from my facial expressions and body posture. How well I regulate my emotional state, tone of voice, and non-verbal cues can help or hinder my son's ability to regulate.

Here is a reminder of some Parenting with Connection principles you may have learned:

- **Regulate your Emotional State**—When your child is out of control, match his or her expressions without matching his emotions. This allows you to communicate to him or her that you understand what he or she is feeling while staying regulated yourself and helping them do the same.

If I don't do this well, my son angrily yells at me, "You're just making fun of me!" He especially does this if he is hurt or upset. I admit that my first reaction is one of two things. I either want to tell him to "Suck it up. You will be okay." or I have to muffle a laugh, because sometimes he is really cute or funny.

Neither reaction matches his emotion, and he usually melts down further. However, if I do a good job of regulating my emotional state and matching his expressions, he feels comforted and understood.

- **Practice Total Voice Control (TVC)**—Let's just say I am terrible at this. I try to use a firm voice, and it comes out as harsh and stern. My son usually responds with fear. He either runs from me or he tries to fight me by hitting, kicking, or throwing something at me. His eyes will dilate and I can see the look of fear.

"Specifically, your voice, and how you use it, matters a great deal when responding to fear-driven responses from your child as well as dealing with misbehavior."— Dr. Purvis

- **T stands for Tone**—Learn the difference between a firm tone and a harsh tone. I think again about Mister Rogers. I should listen to him over and over until I get that calm yet firm sound in my voice along with a less scary face.

- **V stand for Volume**—Notice the loudness or bigness of your voice when correcting. I spent years learning how to project my voice for singing. I use to joke with friends about having the nickname "Larry Loud." I have silenced a roaring room of a few hundred without the use of a microphone more than once. That's not exactly the volume I need to use when talking to my son though.

- **C stands for Cadence**—Slowing the cadence grabs attention and avoids a harsh tone and a loud volume. I have noticed that both Danielle and I tend to talk faster when trying to correct or direct our son. It's like I think I can accomplish this better if I can barrage him with more words or keep talking so he doesn't have any airspace for a sassy or defiant comeback.

My son almost always regulates when I slow down my cadence, use a lower volume, and use an appropriate tone. I can visually see him able to respond to me with cognitive thinking rather than with a fear-based response.

- **Focus on Nonverbal Communication—** Consider not only the words you use or don't use but also your nonverbal signals. Is your posture relaxed and inviting or rigid and threatening?

It really would help if we always had a mirror in front of us especially when we interact with our kids. I know I wouldn't like the reflection of my nonverbal communication.

I only know one way to do this well. I rarely am aware of my nonverbal cues in the moment of interaction with my son, especially if I react with big emotion. What helps me is to put a mirror up to my heart. My emotion, my tone, my nonverbal communications tend to follow the state of my heart.

Sometimes I can do this in the moment, but the best result is when I take time early each day with God. When I invite Him into my day, when I rest in the fact that He is in control, when I allow His Spirit to manifest His peace, joy, kindness, patience, and so on in my heart, my response to my son, and anyone else, reflects that time spent with God.

Regulating our emotional state, including our voice control and nonverbal communication, will help our kids from a hard place regulate their emotions. They need us to be able to do this. They need a healthy brain to model for them how to do this. Besides, how can we can expect them to respond in a healthy manner if we can't ourselves?

I don't know about you but if I am going 90 miles an hour trying to conquer the world, I struggle with regulating myself much less helping anyone else.

In this next chapter I will help you find a healthy pace to life. When you parent kids from a hard place, they need you to be present in their lives. That takes time and energy.

CHAPTER TWENTY-TWO

Structuring Your Life

I sat in a Bible study a few years ago and listened to couple after couple complain about the busyness of their lives. Most families had two working parents and children in multiple activities. Something in our culture convinces us that if we aren't involved in every activity that presents itself, we are somehow missing out.

I kept my mouth shut because I don't think they wanted their lives to change. They just wanted to complain about it. I am not judging them. I understand how it's easy and tempting to slide into that lifestyle.

However, if you are about to foster or adopt a child, please take a look at the pace of your lifestyle and consider slowing it down. Even if you have had foster or adopted children in your family for awhile, if they aren't adjusting well or keep having behavioral challenges, this might be part of the problem.

What to Consider Changing

You know by now that Danielle and I didn't have any children of our own when we decided to foster and adopt. In some ways it was easy to alter our lifestyle to integrate our son into our family. But then again, we had our routines, lots of flexibility, and a pace that we needed to alter.

For example, Danielle and I were used to going out to eat or out with friends at a moment's notice. We never had to worry about getting babysitters or getting home at a certain time. We slept in as late as we wanted when we could. In other words, our day-to-day lifestyle revolved around us.

We also traveled a lot. We took trips for pleasure anytime during the year. And we went on lots of mission trips.

I am not sure we had a grasp on how much our lifestyle would change when we began fostering, but it did, and it wasn't too much different from a family that brings home a newborn—except we only got about a one-hour notice instead of nine months.

Both Danielle and I did go on a mission trip since we adopted our son. I went to Honduras in 2012, and Danielle went to Thailand in 2013. We survived and so did our son, but we decided that we should postpone that part of our lifestyle for a few more years.

You might wonder why we couldn't we keep going on mission trips each year. I guess we could, but understanding that our son experienced abandonment, either of us being gone for 10 to 14 days took its toll on him.

We decided that if we brought him into our family, we would slow down our lifestyle for a little while.

Your lifestyle might look like taking two vacations a year. Both husband and wife work 50 plus hours a week. Each person in the family—you, your spouse, and both of your biological kids—have one or two commitments outside of work and school each week—sports, clubs, volunteering, church, and so on.

The challenge is that we think we can do it all. The reality is that **we can't do it all**. We don't *have* to do it all. Slowing your pace down personally and as a family will take work, but the pain suffered by trying to keep the same pace is much greater.

So you're convinced that you need to slow things down, but you don't know how to do it. Well here are a few ideas:

- **Remember Your Role**

When you decided to foster or adopt, you made a commitment to that child. Part of that commitment was to help your child heal from their past. Part of that past most likely includes uncertainty. Your foster or adopted child needs extra time and a slower pace to process their environments and to feel safe.

One way to fulfill that commitment is to be fully present. That is hard to do if you are constantly on the go, working long hours, spending time taking your other children to many activities, and constantly on your mobile device.

- **Prioritize**

It really takes rearranging your priorities, not just you as the parent but, again, the children too. That is why it is important that your biological children are all in on fostering or adopting. It impacts the entire family.

Either you or your spouse might need to take extended leave or even take a job with less demands. Remember us talking about securing attachment with your foster or adopted child in chapter 2? That first six to 18 months they are in your family, regardless of their age, are crucial to you attaching to them. They need you to spend as much time as you can with them.

- **Postpone Big Changes**

That job change or a move to another house can wait. Yes, it might mean getting passed over for a promotion or remaining content with the house you live in now.

We moved into a new home about five years after our son was placed with us. Even after that length of time, the change unsettled our son for a while.

Maintain as much stability as you possibly can.

- **Learn to Say No**

The fact that you foster or adopt a child tells me a lot about you. You don't shy away from commitments. You take on challenges. You are moved by compassion. And you might even think that you can conquer the world.

But you *can't* do everything. No one can. Learn to say no to that volunteer position at church or school. Say no to the "only one night a week" sports league. You might even need to say no to bringing another child into your family for a few months or longer.

- **Remember It's a Season**

Just like anything, it won't always be this way, unless your child has high needs. But even if they do, either physically or mentally, you hopefully will reach a level of stability and predictability so that you can begin to add some things back into your lifestyle.

After about a year, I began playing in a sports league again. I fully expect that Danielle and I will begin going on more mission trips again.

So when you do slow things down, it probably will be for only a season.

- **Recruit a Team**

I am not sure why foster and adoptive parents tend to try to do it all on their own, but we do.

When CPS placed our son with us, they told us that it was for only a few weeks. So when different friends offered to get certified for respite care, we told them that we didn't need them to do that. To this day I am not sure why that was our reply. If he had only been with us for a few weeks, we planned on fostering other children.

Put a team around you that includes those who are certified for respite care, those who will bring meals (even at the last minute), others who will go shopping for you, and so on.

The main objective is to create or maintain a pace that allows you margin to handle unexpected or challenging times. You know that they happen. You can't control what your child is going through or how they will handle it. You can control, however, if you have the time and energy to be fully present with your child to help them make sense of their life and to heal from their past.

One thing that makes this challenging for us as parents is what we bring to the relationship. We need to know our history, maybe even of trauma, our attachment style, why some things push our buttons, and our expectations. All these things affect our kids' ability to heal.

In the next chapter we will discover what it looks like to pay attention to what you bring. You won't want to miss an interview with Marshall Lyles about our attachment styles and our own trauma and how that impacts our parenting.

CHAPTER TWENTY-THREE

Paying Attention to What You Bring

I enjoy those little survey questions that my son brought home from preschool where he answered questions about me and Danielle. Things like "What is your daddy's job? What is your mommy's favorite food? and How old are your mommy and daddy?"

According to our son, I am 500 years old, and Danielle is 1,000 years old. I'm not sure where he got that, but he thinks that we are *really* old.

He looks at me with amazement when I tell him stories of when I was a little boy or a teenager. Sometimes when I tell him about places that Danielle and I have visited or lived, he will ask me, "Was that before I was born?" or "Was that before I was a part of your family?" "Yes son it sure was."

He knows at some level that we have lived longer and experienced more life than he has, but he has no idea what we really bring to our relationship.

The question, is do I really know what I am bringing to the relationship?

We all are very good at having a short memory or blocking out things from our past. Even if that is true, we all bring our own history, motivations, and expectations into the relationship.

When we understand this and we are willing to pay attention to it, even work on it, it helps us to show our kids the way to healing.

Dr. Curt Thompson, author of *Anatomy of the Soul*, says it like this: "Pay attention to what you are actually paying attention to." In other words, do you pay attention to your "default mode" of responding to your child's behavior?

Does Your History Affect Your Parenting?

Our childhood, our relationships, our past hurts, and our successes all play a part in the way we parent our children.

Are you aware how all that history impacts your relationship with your child? If you overreact to your child when they push your buttons, it is probably more about your stuff than theirs.

One part of our history is how well our own relational and emotional needs have been met. Are you aware that you have these needs? How in touch with them are you? How well do you communicate these to people in your life that can meet these needs?

I include here a list of 10 emotional needs that is taught by Intimate Life Ministries. See if you can identify your top three.

1. **Acceptance**—This involves looking beyond faults, differences, and irritations to see worth.

2. **Affection**—This includes verbalizing "I care for you" and "I'm here for you" and can be both nonsexual and sexual.

3. **Appreciation**—Not taking things for granted and looking for the best rather than pointing out the flaws is all part of appreciation.

4. **Approval**—Approval involves recognizing the special things about a person and thanking them for who they are.

5. **Attention**—Attention is taking time to listen, remembering to tell each other about the day, and interest without criticism.

6. **Comfort**—This is sensitively showing concern about another's disappointment or hurt and hurting with or for another's pain.

7. **Encouragement**—This involves helping a person to keep going when enthusiasm is gone and not rushing in to take over a task when encouragement would result in the task being completed.

8. **Respect**—Respect is honoring each other, never putting each other down in front of others, and

being willing to be serious when a joke would be hurtful and imply criticism.

9. **Security**—Security is knowing that security is found in strong, reliable relationships, and doing the little things with consistency.

10. **Support**—This is letting others know that you can be counted on, noticing times of particular stress and offering help, and sharing tasks.

The reason this is important is because when those needs go unmet, you react in needy ways. If you have unmet emotional needs happening and that collides with your child's needs, then you have chaos.

Knowing what your needs are and communicating them in healthy ways to those who can meet them, like your spouse, will help you to have room to meet the needs your child has.

What Is Your Attachment Style?

A lot is written about the attachment style of children, but we parents also have an attachment style. We often overlook how that affects our relationship with our children.

We talked about helping our kids earn a secure attachment in Chapter 2. Take a look back to remind yourself about the four attachment styles. Which attachment style do you have? There is not a right or wrong answer, only an accurate one. How willing are you to accurately assess yourself?

When things get tough, you will usually default to your original attachment style.

I recognized that I default to a dismissive style, which means I will pull away when things get hard—not exactly what my son who experienced abandonment needs from me. Instead I need to work on staying fully present. If I do that, my son has a better chance of learning how to relate and respond in relationships.

To help gain a better understanding about how our own attachment styles impact our parenting, listen to an interview with Marshall Lyles (www.kennethacamp.com/session5). Marshall serves as the Director of Training at the Center for Relational Care in Austin, Texas. Most of his clinical practice focuses on attachment trauma and its effect on family relationships.

Here are a few takeaways from the interview:

- All of us are somewhere on the spectrum of healing when it comes to attachment.

- When we bring a wounded child into our home, we bring them into contact with our own wounds.

- If we as parents have a humility about who we are and what we need, it can open up profound opportunities to help your children heal. Marshall calls this having a compassionate curiosity about your own story.

- One red flag Marshall shared—how am I telling the story of my own childhood?

You can hear the entire interview by going to www.kennethacamp.com/session5.

Own Your Stuff

When we encounter behavioral challenges and conflict with our children, it is important that we ask these important questions: What part of this is really about me? Which of my buttons are being pushed? Why does this bother me?

Keep in mind that just because your own stuff may be getting in the way, it does not mean that you ignore or excuse wrong behaviors. Neither does it mean that you fail to correct. But it does mean that you need to be aware of what you are contributing to the dynamic and then be willing to admit your part in it and begin to address it so that you can be more fully available to meet your child's needs and move forward together.

I find myself doing this in *real time* with my son. For example, a few years ago our neighbors who had two kids about our sons age moved to California. At three years old, my son didn't know how to process this change, so he acted out in different ways—clingy/separation anxiety, chewing on his clothing, deliberate disobedience, etc. Boy, did his behavior push my buttons.

Part of my struggle, a big part of it, was my own stuff.

Many times I can see how I am reacting poorly to him (or I notice my wife's look.). Sometimes I can change my behavior or pay attention to how I am responding in order to stay in the moment with my son. This helps him regulate and relate better. Then other times either I have to remove myself from the situation or just watch it all blow up

Expectations

> "All parents bring expectations with them into parenting—some realistic and others not. For adoptive families, however, lingering unrealistic expectations can lead to disappointment, frustration and even a real disconnection between parents and children. When a child's history of pain and loss begins to taint the beautiful picture of what a parent expected their adoption journey to look like, parents are tempted to protect their image rather than embrace their child's feelings and struggles. When a child's behaviors (rooted in fear and an instinct to survive) begin to collide with the 'way we do things as a family' and are only made worse by a parent's attempts at discipline, parents can find themselves exhausted and quickly nearing the point of despair."
> —Empowered to Connect

"Parents are tempted to protect their image rather than embrace their child's feelings and struggles." OUCH! I am often more interested in my agenda, my feelings, and my needs than my adopted child's.

Evaluating our motivations too is important because out of these flow our expectations. This is true for any relationship.

Jayne Schooler, author of Wounded Children, Healing Homes: How Traumatized Children Impact Adoptive and Foster Families, writes about how foster and adoptive families form unrealistic expectations with what she calls the Model of the Myth, which consists of the following five steps:

1. **Something is learned.** For example statistics are given about foster care in your community.

2. **Information is filtered and something is believed.** After Danielle and I heard these statistics, we believed that we needed to consider fostering.

3. **Expectations form based on the filtered information and resulting belief.** We expected any child we fostered or especially adopted to appreciate their better life.

4. **Unrealistic expectations fail.** In our case, we had an eight-month-old foster son placed with us that we eventually adopted when he was two. Of

course, he had no ability at this age to express appreciation.

5. **Unmet expectations result in conflict, disappointment, discouragement, and despair.** One of the biggest challenges in our home has been our son's difficulty with attaching to or showing compassion toward Danielle.

When we experience this model, the question is, how do we respond? Do we point the finger at our child or back at our unrealistic expectations? It's not a matter of lowering our expectations; it is simply about setting your expectations appropriately.

Our target is arriving at being fully present and attuned with our child not allowing our past or future expectations to hinder our goal. Easier said than done. And it doesn't happen overnight or without error.

I know that was a lot to digest, but it's so important to pay attention to what we bring to the equation. The better we do this, the better we can help our kids.

So are you paying attention to how well you are taking care of yourself? Danielle and I slipped into a pattern that ignored our emotional, spiritual, and physical health. Read on to discover some ways you can take care of yourself.

CHAPTER TWENTY-FOUR

Taking Care of Yourself

Our foster agency caseworker told me on the phone that the eight-month-old boy that CPS needed to place would probably be with us for only a couple of weeks. So I agreed to the placement thinking that I could do anything for a couple of weeks.

That was June 2011. July, August, and September went by and he still lived with us. He turned one year-old in October. I really had thought that he would go back to someone in his biological family in time to celebrate his first birthday.

We celebrated that first birthday. Chocolate cake smeared over his baby face. Eyes full of delight as he opened some presents.

With the holidays on the horizon, we thought surely things would work out for him to spend Thanksgiving or at the very least Christmas back with his biological family.

At a court hearing in the middle of November, the judge decided against that. Our son's biological grandmother met me in the hallway, sadness etched on her face, to let me know that she had Christmas presents in the car.

This state of not knowing what the next day held continued for another several months until we adopted our son in September 2012, the month before he turned two.

The point of all that is that Danielle and I got stuck in the mode of "we can do anything for a few weeks" for over a year. What happened is that we completely put on the shelf the importance of taking care of ourselves individually and our marriage.

We fell into a pattern that a lot of foster and adoptive parents fall into. We feel that our child's needs are more important than our needs. We fail to recognize that taking care of ourselves will ensure that we have what we need to give to our kids.

That's usually where our training breaks down. We may know Parenting with Connection principles inside and out. We might even teach them to others, but if we don't take care of ourselves everything will eventually fall apart.

Does this sound like you, your family, or your marriage? Are you so consumed with the needs of your child that you ignore your own needs? Do you put your child's cry for help above what your spouse needs?

I understand. In the moment, when you have one or more children in your home who come from such brokenness, you convince yourself that you don't have time to eat right, get enough exercise and rest, or work on your marriage.

That is a big mistake.

Your child needs you to take care of yourself too. Your child needs your marriage to stay strong. My son draws from the level of connection that Danielle and I have for each other. The better health I personally am in and the healthier our marriage is, the better environment it is for my son to feel safe and heal.

How can we take care of ourselves when we have so many demands on our time, emotions, and mental energy so that we can be fully present for our kids?

- **Pay attention to your body.**

We talk about helping our children learn self-awareness all of the time. We help them identify when they are hungry, thirsty, or tired. Then we teach them words to communicate to others who can help them. We help them learn what the big feelings they have are called and how to handle them in healthy ways.

But how good are we at doing that for ourselves?

I need regular physical activity or I get sad, even depressed. Remember the chapter about getting your child moving? It applies to us as parents too. I do things that I enjoy like playing basketball, going for walks, and even working on our property. These things help keep me in somewhat good shape, and they also help change my brain chemistry.

Another way to take care of your body is to eat well and consistently. When we are constantly on the go, we can grab whatever whenever and shove it in our mouth. It pays off to take the time to eat as healthy as possible. I even pay attention to how much water I drink during the day.

- **Pay attention to your emotional cup.**

We talked about this in the previous chapter, so I won't go into detail, but I have never been very good at this. I bet I am not alone, so I think it's worth mentioning again. If my emotional cup is full, I will not have any room left to handle my son's emotions.

Take time to do things that will meet your emotional and relational needs that empty your cup. Most of the time that will mean investing in your meaningful relationships

- **Invest in relationships.**

It is too easy to neglect your marriage (if you are married). Days slip into weeks, then months, maybe even into years without any deep relational interaction other than your kids. You and your spouse merely co-exist as you take care of the tasks of keeping the family afloat.

You recognize that isn't healthy, but it might easily describe your family.

We are created to relate with others, deeply. We *need* connection. But it takes effort to make it happen. I know you are investing in your kids, but I urge you to make it a focus to spend time with your spouse.

After we adopted our son, Danielle and I realized we needed to prioritize time together. We began by scheduling a date night at least once a month. Sometimes we fully enjoyed each other's company. Other times we wondered why we even tried. The bottom line though is that we spent time connecting.

It is important to invest in other relationships as well. If you are a single parent of a foster or adopted child, please do this.

I have four men that know me well. I make it a point to get together with them often and regularly. I meet a couple of friends weekly. They pour into my life. They listen to me. They help meet my top relational needs.

Another important relationship that I prioritize is with God. I believe that we are spiritual beings created by a personal God. He is the one who created us with the need to connect. Not only are we created to connect with other people but He created us to connect with Him as well.

- **Recruit help.**

I know I have already talked about this as well, but it's so important that we need to hear it again.

We all need breaks from parenting so that we can recharge our batteries, especially if our kids are young. If you are a foster parent, please enlist people who can give you respite. You are not shirking your responsibility. Even if you are an adoptive family, let family and friends give you breaks.

Find a group of like-minded parents who understand the challenges of parenting a child from a hard place and do life with them. Not just online but in person where you get to see the ugly along with the beautiful. We tend to catch how to parent with connection.

Don't overlook professional help. I know that for some of you that is the last thing you will do. You either say that you have plenty of support in other areas or you don't have the money. However, a counselor will tell you things that a friend or support group might not. They can give you objective feedback too.

When our son was about four years old, I was overreacting to him with anger. A lot. I know most parents get angry at their children. That's a human, emotional response. But I overreacted with anger at just about everything my son did or didn't do. I knew that I had some issues that needed addressing, so I went to a trusted counselor who helped me process some things.

Your child might not need a counselor. Who they need the most is a healthy you. *You* might be the one who needs to meet with a counselor so you can be that healthy parent.

- **Understand secondhand trauma.**

We all probably understand that our kids experienced trauma. What goes overlooked is how parents can experience secondhand trauma through interacting with our kids and helping them process and heal.

This goes back to the importance of relationships that can help us stay centered. Otherwise we can find ourselves caught up in the vortex of our child's trauma. They need us at our best to help them make sense of their history, to heal, and to learn how to relate well with others.

This topic, taking care of yourself, is so important that I asked Robyn Gobbel to join me in an interview. Robyn is a licensed clinical social worker and physco-therapist. She speaks and trains often on this subject. In this interview she not only helps us understand the importance of self care, but she also offers practical tips and ideas.

You can listen to this interview by going here – www.kennethacamp.com/session007.

I hope these last four chapters have helped and that it motivates you to pay attention to your emotional state, your pace of life, and what you bring to the relationship so that you can take care of yourself. Remember if you aren't available and fully present for your kid, they can't learn how to securely attach and connect.

CONCLUSION

I admire you! As a foster and/or adoptive parent, you chose to not only bring a child who needed a family into your family but you committed to help a child heal. That child might be in your family for only a few days or for the rest of their lives. It doesn't matter.

The fact that you read this book tells me that you didn't just stop at the front door. You didn't make the decision to welcome a child from a hard place into your home and then go on with life like normal.

No, you understand, maybe through some pain, that this child needs for you to learn how to parent with connection.

It didn't take me long at all to realize that even if my son was in our family for a short time, the only way I could parent him well was if I did two things.

First, I had to learn to stay in the moment. Since he was a foster-only kid, I didn't know from day to day whether he would still be in our family.

Here is how I said it in my book about our foster and adoption journey, *Adopting the Father's Heart*:

> *"The only way I knew how to love him as my own son, knowing that if he left our family someday my heart would break, was to stay in the moment. What I mean is that I had to stay focused on that day, that moment even. If I began to worry about what might happen in the future, I could not fully love him in the present."*

The other thing I needed to do was to parent him as if he was my own flesh and blood. Of course the longer he remained in our family the more that felt natural. But if I didn't do this, then it was like I was a paid child care worker, not a father. Both staying in the moment and parenting as if he was my own biological son helped me to connect with him.

Why am I telling you these two things? Because as you know, foster care and adoption are hard. And if we can't stay in the moment and be all in on the relationship, then we get overwhelmed. When we get overwhelmed, or even get hurt, we will look for a way out.

That is the last thing these kids need. They have already suffered loss, trauma, neglect, and abandonment. They desperately need loving adults who will stay with them through both the good and bad times.

I hope you will add this book to your toolbox. But we don't have to part ways here.

Connect with me at www.KennethACamp.com to access past blog articles, get the current blogs, and listen to invaluable podcast interviews like the ones you linked to here from the book.

One more thing. Be sure to check out the Resource section. There you will find other great websites, podcasts, books, and so on.

Will you do me one favor before you put this book down? Please go here to the Amazon page and leave a raving review. Seriously, any review you give is helpful, but of course a four- or five-star review is greatly appreciated if you think the book warrants it.

ENDNOTES

i. From "Sharing Power with Your Child" video (https://vimeo.com/12521852)

ii. https://www.gottman.com

iii. From Dr. Karyn Purvis and the TCU Institute of Child Development

RESOURCES

Books:

The Connected Child by Purvis and Cross

The Whole Brain Child by Siegel and Bryson

The Out of Sync Child by Kranowitz and Miller

Anatomy of the Soul by Thompson

Nurturing Adoptions by Gray

Attaching in Adoption by Gray

Websites:

Empowered to Connect – www.EmpoweredtoConnect.org

TCU Institute of Child Development – www.child.tcu.edu

Circle of Security – www.circleofsecurity.net

Star Institute for Sensory Processing Disorder – www.spdstar.org

Creative Therapies with Marti Smith – www.creativetherapies.com

ww.sensorysmarts.com

www.sensorydigest.com

www.officeplayground.com

Websites for interviewees:

Marti Smith, OTR/L:
Creative Therapies with Marti Smith –
www.creativetherapies.com

Marshall Lyles, LPC-S, LMFT-S, RPT-S:
www.marshalllyles.com

Center for Relational Care –
www.relationalcare.org

Robyn Gobbel, LCSW:
www.gobbelcounseling.com

Central Texas Attachment and Trauma Center –
www.centraltexasattachmenttrauma.com

Suzette Lamb, LPC-S:
Central Texas Attachment and Trauma Center –
www.centraltexasattachmenttrauma.com

Imbedded podcast links:

Helping Our Son Handle Transitions (with Kenneth and Danielle) – www.kennethacamp.com/Episode6

The Circle of Security: An Interview with Suzette Lamb – www.kennethacamp.com/session009

The Struggle to Attach (with Kenneth and Danielle) – www.kennethacamp.com/Episode12

Implementing Time In (with Kenneth and Danielle) – www.kennethacamp.com/TimeIn

Understanding Your Child's Sensory Processing Needs: An Interview with Marti Smith – www.kennethacamp.com/session8

How Our Attachment Style Impacts Our Parenting: An Interview with Marshall Lyles – www.kennethacamp.com/session5

The Importance of Parental Self Care: An Interview with Robyn Gobbel – www.kennethacamp.com/session007

ACKNOWLEDGEMENTS

Many contributed to this book! Thank you Carie and Sandra for sharing stories from your heart about your journey of foster care and adoption. Samir, Dawn, Danielle, and Sandra, thank you for taking time to read through my very first terrible rough drafts. You helped me to process my thoughts.

Also, a huge thank you to Robyn Gobbel, Marshall Lyles, Suzette Lamb, and Marti Smith for taking time to record podcast interviews. Your expertise and passion for families and hurting kids helps and encourages each of them.

Shout out to Daphne Parsekian for editing the book and Jen Henderson for formatting the book. I enjoyed working with you both!

To everyone who has helped spread the word about this book—I greatly appreciate each one of you!

My biggest thanks goes to my wife Danielle who continues to walk with me in this never-boring journey God has us on. Not only do you cheerlead me as I write and create content, you also have a husband and a son who think you are the best Mom in the world.

ABOUT THE AUTHOR

Kenneth A Camp is an adoptive father, missionary, blogger, and podcaster. He is the author of two related books, *Adopting the Father's Heart* and *Respond to the Call to Care for Orphans: Count the Cost.* He served on the boards for Partners in Hope Lake Travis and Canyon Creek Preschool. He currently serves on the board of Fostering Hope Austin.

Kenneth's blog articles have been featured on The Forgotten Initiative and Foster2Forever websites. He and his wife, Danielle, are also certified trainers for Empowered to Connect, a training based on parenting with connection principles taught by TCU Institute of Child Development.

Kenneth has also served as a youth pastor, a missions pastor, and with Danielle, a missionary in Thailand. Kenneth and Danielle are the parents of one son they adopted from foster care and reside outside of Austin, Texas.

Thank you for purchasing my book! I really appreciate all of your feedback, and I love hearing what you have to say.

I need your input to make the next version better.

Please leave me a helpful REVIEW on Amazon.

Thanks so much!!

Kenneth A Camp

SELF-PUBLISHING
SCHOOL

NOW IT'S YOUR TURN

Discover the EXACT 3-step blueprint you need to become a bestselling author in 3 months.

Self-Publishing School helped me, and now I want them to help you with this FREE VIDEO SERIES!

Even if you're busy, bad at writing, or don't know where to start, you CAN write a bestseller and build your best life.

With tools and experience across a variety niches and professions, Self-Publishing School is the only resource you need to take your book to the finish line!

DON'T WAIT

Watch this FREE VIDEO SERIES now, and Say "YES" to becoming a bestseller:

Self-Publishing Video Series
(https://xe172.isrefer.com/go/curcust/kennethcamp) *This is an affiliate link

Made in United States
North Haven, CT
02 April 2022

17806835R00111